Instructional Programming:
Issues and Innovations in School Scheduling

Instructional Programming:
Issues and Innovations in School Scheduling

ANTHONY SAVILLE
University of Nevada,
Las Vegas

CHARLES E. MERRILL PUBLISHING COMPANY
A Bell & Howell Company
Columbus, Ohio 43216

THE CHARLES E. MERRILL
PRINCIPALSHIP IN LEADERSHIP PERSPECTIVE SERIES
Under the Editorship of
Stephen J. Knezevich

Published by
CHARLES E. MERRILL PUBLISHING COMPANY
A Bell and Howell Company
Columbus, Ohio 43216

International Standard Book Number:
0-675-09064-4

Library of Congress Card Catalog Number:
72-84125

Printed in the United States of America

to my wife,
Joy Lee Randolph Saville

Preface

One of the most demanding assignments facing the modern-day principal is the integration and application of organizational concepts as they relate to the daily operation of a school. He not only must deal with the sociological, psychological, and theoretical aspects of a changing society but must also be able to perform competently the technical-managerial tasks confronting him at all times.

The principal is not only an educational leader in a collegial sense but is also an organizational engineer in a managerial sense. One of his key organizational tasks is the development of the daily schedule. Another is the maintenance of an accurate and well-publicized school calendar.

This era of change demands that the principal fundamentally operate from sound basic principles of educational leadership. The "nuts and bolts" factors utilize these principles as a springboard for application. Although the materials presented in this book are primarily "how-to-do-it" with respect to constructing school schedules and calendars, they have been based on principles of educational administration drawn from the research and experience of many.

The purpose of this volume, therefore, is to assist those new "middle-management" administrators operating at all grade levels by providing ideas and concepts relating to these particular facets of their assignment. It also has been designed to forward information about new scheduling concepts and variations used by many schools as an aid to principals who are interested in revising, adapting, or rebuilding their scheduling systems.

Anthony Saville

Contents

CHAPTER ONE

THE PROGRAMMING OR SCHEDULING OF LEARNING
EXPERIENCES   1

CHAPTER TWO

REGISTRATION: PROCEDURES GOVERNING THE
LEARNER'S ENTRY INTO ELEMENTARY AND
SECONDARY SCHOOL OPPORTUNITIES   15

CHAPTER THREE

THE MASTER SCHEDULE: THE COMPREHENSIVE PROGRAMMING INSTRUMENT 43

CHAPTER FOUR

SCHEDULING INSTRUCTIONAL ACTIVITIES IN THE ELEMENTARY SCHOOL 61

CHAPTER FIVE

SCHEDULING INSTRUCTIONAL ACTIVITIES IN THE SECONDARY SCHOOL 87

CHAPTER SIX

FLEXIBLE PROGRAMMING AND COMPUTER-BASED
APPROACHES 123

CHAPTER SEVEN

PROGRAMMING EXPERIENCES DURING THE
SCHOOL YEAR: TRENDS AND ISSUES IN SCHOOL
CALENDAR DEVELOPMENT 165

CHAPTER EIGHT

PROGRAMMING THE EXTENDED SCHOOL YEAR 175

CHAPTER NINE

NEW HORIZONS   *211*

INDEX   *215*

Illustrations

CHAPTER THREE

CHAPTER FOUR

CHAPTER FIVE

CHAPTER SIX

CHAPTER SEVEN

CHAPTER EIGHT

Chapter One

The Programming or Scheduling of Learning Experiences

Elementary and secondary schools in the U.S. are complex social institutions offering a comprehensive range of learning opportunities. The realization of these educational objectives demands coordination of a wide variety of inputs, such as time, talents, materials, and facilities. From the moment the learner presents himself for registration for his initial entry into the school until he terminates with a high school diploma, someone must assume the operational challenge of organizing the total spectrum of instructional resources in the learner's behalf. More often than not, the person responsible for the effective and efficient management of instructional time, talents, materials, and facilities is the school principal. However, new technology, fresh insights into the nature of learning, and changing value patterns have served to compound the problems faced by the principal as he develops instructional programming for students.

The concept of instructional programming can be explained as the process of arranging discrete learning experiences within a time frame and in a sequence appropriate to the needs of the learner and consistent with the constraints imposed upon the institution. In addition, student learning must be guided by *someone* at *some place.* The most efficient utilization and coor-

1

dination of all these educational factors in a logical sequence comprises the substance of instructional programming. Such work is more than a pedestrian or purely mechanical chore. It is a creative challenge made more so by the availability of new insights into educational operations as well as by new technology.

Instructional programming is similar in substance to what is more traditionally called *school scheduling*. Scheduling demands the development of a detailed plan for the utilization of a given set of resources or procedures at any given time. Some educators argue that programming focuses on sequencing while scheduling emphasizes timing.

In its broadest definition, however, programming includes the timing and sequence of learning resources to achieve educational missions just as does scheduling. For that reason, the term instructional programming will be used as a synonym for school scheduling for the purposes of this volume.

The units of time allocated to any given learning experience will vary with the maturity of the learner in question as well as with the structure of the discipline, type of skill to be developed, and the teacher's instructional strategy. Experiences may be programmed within the time frame defined as the school day, school week, or school year. A *school calendar* is the term most often used to specify instructional programming of a rather general type during the school year. The *school schedule* is the end result of daily and/or weekly programming of instructional activities. The time frame on a daily basis may vary from a unit or module as short as twelve or fifteen minutes, to the more traditional period of about fifty minutes, and even to large blocks of time of several hours or more. Instructional programming, or school scheduling, is an important dimension of school operations, for it has a significant impact on the learner, the interaction between teacher and learner, and the methods of teaching used to promote acquisition of a given concept or skill.

A prime managerial responsibility of the school principal is the programming, or scheduling, of curricular experiences offered in his attendance unit. The task of verifying that a schedule is accurate, informative, relevant, and flexible is a major technical challenge. The onslaught of new technology, such as computer-based scheduling, merely reinforces this challenge, for the school principal must be able to correlate the many intricacies of machines with the increasingly complex and self-seeking human being.

According to David Austin; Will French; and J. Dan Hull, the principal's task of relating all of these elements

> ... requires skill in careful planning, in being sensitive to the individual and the group needs, in developing good decisions in harmony with the goals and purposes of the school, and in a continuing study of the results obtained. Somewhere about each school—and usually near the principal's office—will be found a formal record of the coordination of students, staff, space and time. This is the "master schedule" of that school.[1]

ADMINISTRATIVE RESPONSIBILITY FOR THE SCHOOL SCHEDULE

Regardless of the size or grade level of the school, the planning of the daily instructional program is a difficult assignment. Since it affects all students, faculty, and non-certified personnel, all of these people must be included in the total planning procedure. In smaller schools, the principal often assumes sole responsibility for planning and constructing the schedule. Although he may consult teachers regarding time and room preference or students and facilities desired, he generally performs the task of structuring the schedule himself, without any further faculty involvement. Too often, this failure to broaden faculty participation to include assignment and load creates needless confusion and apprehension among teachers.

In larger schools, the principal may delegate the programming of instructional activities to an assistant principal or counselor. In some instances, a scheduling committee composed of faculty, counselors, and administrative personnel function as a

---

[1]David B. Austin; Will French; and J. Dan Hull, *American High School Administration*, 3rd ed (New York: Holt, Rinehart, and Winston, 1962), p. 294. Reprinted by permission of the publisher.

team in their attempt to include all related factors in the final product—the daily schedule. Sometimes, the students themselves are directly involved in constructing the daily pattern of instructional activities through the "Daily Demand System" that will be described in more detail in Chapter Six.

Instructional programming within the context of the self-contained elementary school classrooms is quite different from scheduling departmentalized secondary school classes. Because the middle school shows characteristics of both organizational patterns, the elementary principal in the more innovative instructional organizational patterns finds it necessary to familiarize himself with departmentalized scheduling. Consequently, administering the schedule in the *modern school* requires a consideration of some principles of operation that are common to all grade levels.

Experience and research make one point vividly clear. Teachers themselves should be directly involved in planning and administrating the school schedule in all types of schools. Ideally, principals, both elementary and secondary, would submit their preliminary schedules to faculty reactions. Each teacher would be requested to review and approve his individual pattern of instruction or classes for the current or coming year, indicating his final approval by initialing the Master Schedule.

ELEMENTS AFFECTING INSTRUCTIONAL PROGRAMMING

Several key factors control how the school schedule is structured and operated. Although these factors are identified in the following paragraphs, they will be discussed in detail later as they relate to a specific program.

Determining Policies.   Before actual construction of the schedule can be undertaken, certain basic policy decisions concerning the various components of the school program must be made. Bent and McCann, in *Administration of Secondary Schools,* suggest resolution of the following policy decisions as necessary prerequisites to scheduling. These broadly stated policies apply to the elementary school program as well.

1. The specific courses to be offered in a school program.
2. The organization of the curriculum—whether on an activity or core basis, or on an individual subject basis.
3. The organization of the school day; the hours of sessions, the length of periods, use of double periods and large blocks of time, and noon-hour plans.
4. The impact of double extended school sessions, if these are in use.
5. The effect of collegiate attendance plans (under which high school students attend only those classes for which they are scheduled during the school day and need not remain at school at other hours), if these are in use.
6. The use of semi-annual promotions.
7. The influence of work experiences and other extended school programs.
8. The use of the activity period for meeting of school clubs, journalism groups, musical organizations, athletic practice, and others.
9. The operation of homeroom and assembly periods.
10. Normal and permitted subject loads for students.
11. Pupils assignments for study-hall, library, or guidance periods.
12. Required subjects generally or in each specific curriculum.
13. Maximum and minimum size of classes permitted in the various subjects taught.
14. Methods of assigning pupils to class sections, whether on the basis of homogeneous sex, curriculum elected, or otherwise.
15. Policies on the control of class interruptions and schedule irregularities.[2]

Philosophy and Curriculum.   A comprehensive study of district and school philosophies should be conducted prior to determining the year's course offerings. Questions such as *What is the purpose of the school program?* and *Why are certain subjects offered?* should be clearly answered before the curriculum is involved. Obviously, state laws mandate the inclusion of certain subjects by grade level and minimum time requirements for the school day. Some states specify the exact grade

---

[2]Rudyard K. Bent and Lloyd E. McCann, *Administration of Secondary Schools* (New York: McGraw Hill Book Company, Inc., 1960), p. 207. Reprinted by permission of the publisher.

level at which certain disciplines are to be taught, while others allow schools to use discretion in interpreting the laws and in offering the courses when they appear to be most applicable in the local school system. Time is one of the major controlling components at the state level. In the elementary school, state education department policies or laws may stipulate the minimum number of minutes per year to be allocated to each subject. At the secondary level, the Carnegie unit, or some variation of it, may be the basic determinant. The Carnegie unit is based on a minimum number of minutes (forty-five) for a minimum number of class meetings per week in one subject (five) over the school year.

Many state departments of education have encouraged experimentation. It usually is not too difficult for a school to request a change in operations from the chief state school offices and receive approval for experimentation.

Enrollment.   Enrollment figures are necessary in planning the sequence of instructional activities for the school year. These figures provide the basic data essential for computing the number of teachers, space, facilities and materials required to operate the program effectively. Various sources of enrollment data are available for calculating enrollment projections, and, usually, combinations of these sources are utilized to obtain a reasonably accurate projection. In stable communities, there is less concern about accuracy than in districts where two-thirds of the school population may be migrant and enrollment figures are a challenging variable to predict. At present, there is no simple formula or technique for solving this dilemma, and for that reason predicted enrollment ranges may be necessary.

The major *sources of enrollment data* available to school attendance personnel may be identified as:

District Enrollment Figures and Projections.   Most school districts maintain records of past enrollments, and many have developed three-to ten-year projections as an aid to planning programs and facilities for the future. Although in some cases the figures in these projections are too global to apply in an individual school, they may suggest trends or even growth ratios. Districtwide data on feeder schools should be of considerable value to the secondary-level units.

Population Figures. Population projections obtained from census figures and community studies of growth patterns are of value in establishing or corroborating trends or ratios in computing the school enrollment figures for the district as a whole or within a given attendance area.

Average Daily Attendance. Perhaps the most accurate means of determining enrollment figures in an individual school is to review the patterns established in that school during the preceding three-to-five year period. The following formula will indicate that the trend and actual figures can be computed by formula. Glen Ovard suggests that these figures can be calculated by using the following formula, which is applicable to any grade level:

> Estimated Seventh-Grade Enrollment = Sixth-Grade
> Enrollment ±Average Difference of Progression
> from Sixth to Seventh Grade
> over a Three- to Five-Year Period[3]

Feeder Schools. Frequently, in the seventh or eighth grades and particularly in the ninth grades, the feeder effect from both public and private elementary schools must be considered. The impact of private schools in the community upon a particular grade-level enrollment is sometimes neglected, thereby resulting in unexpected scheduling problems after the schedule has been constructed.

A form or chart should be designed to assist in computing this effect. Figure 1.1. illustrates a procedure one might use to calculate enrollments prior to preparing the daily schedule.

---

[3]Glen F. Ovard, *Administration of the Changing Secondary School* (New York: The Macmillan Company, 1966), p. 167. Copyright © by Glen F. Ovard, 1966. Reprinted by permission of the publisher and author.

Date_____			
Current Enrollments			
Ninth Grades	*Boys*	*Girls*	*Total*
A Junior H.S.	____	____	____
B Junior H.S.	____	____	____
C Junior H.S.	____	____	____
Totals			
Loss through retention	____	____	____
Drop Outs	____	____	____
In-migration	____	____	____
(In minus out migration)	____	____	____
Totals			
Predicted 10th Grade	____	____	____

FIGURE 1.1. Chart for Calculating Enrollments.

This chart can be continued by using the same procedure for the tenth and eleventh grades. If a school system uses an eight-four pattern or some other variation, the work sheet should be adjusted to apply to that particular pattern. Once the enrollment figures are established, the class sizes and staff can be calculated.

Class-Size Policy.   Certain policy decisions pertaining to class-size and student-faculty ratios should be agreed upon before schedule construction begins. Some of the factors serving as a basis for policy determinates are listed below.

1. *National or state recommendations.* An example of such a recommendation is Conant's suggestion that a secondary English teacher work with no more than 100 students per day. Over thirty states provide foundation financing which controlls class-size units.

2. *The philosophy of the district and administration.* Some groups argue for large classes using economy as the basis of their decision. Others, if not restricted by limited

finances, attempt to use some learning theory or curriculum philosophy to determine class-size decisions.

3. *Building capacity and special facilities.* Lack of space may force increases in class size or even force schools to operate on double sessions. Limited service or special facilities also have a direct effect upon class-size scheduling.

4. *Teacher organization or union standards.* These factors now are being interjected rather forcefully via negotiations or collective bargaining sessions in some schools.

5. *Fiscal considerations.*

6. *Faculty.* Both the number and qualifications of available faculty are major considerations.

7. *Experimental or nonconventional programs.* These programs may require additional staff, funds, or time. For example, teachers may be transferred from regular assignments to assist with a research project. Such a case could influence the size of classes in conventional programs.

8. *Class load definition.* Class size often is directly affected by what the district or individual school defines as class load. Methods for determining class load will be discussed in depth in Chapter Four.

SPECIAL FACTORS AFFECTING SCHEDULES

Innovation. Whenever a special project or program is planned, the conventional schedule is immediately affected. Certain types of special projects, such as individualization of instruction and differentiation of programs (including special education), require structures which become organizational vehicles for new programs. Nongraded classes and team-teaching with modular scheduling are but two examples of this phenomenon.

Time. In conventional schools, the length of the class period, module, and double laboratory periods create the greatest problems in allocating time. The introduction of flexible (modular) scheduling has created a particular demand for different procedures for schedule construction and time factor considerations.

The overcrowding of schools has required extended school days and even double sessions in many areas. Requests for longer periods of teacher-supervised study in the classroom have brought about lengthened class periods or blocks of time for work-study and even play.

Teacher Preparation.   The current trend in teacher preparation is toward developing teachers with strong backgrounds in the disciplines to be taught. A large number of colleges of education now require the minimum of an academic minor even for elementary teachers. A few universities have organized graduate schools of education which offer the professional preparation to future teachers at the fifth year or master's degree level. Because of their academic background and concentrated professional training, these teachers are prepared to move directly into departmentalized and specialized programs, particularly at the middle school and elementary levels. The principal must consider this new breed of teacher in developing the school schedule.

Teacher Load.   A major area of concern for teachers is the identification and weighting of factors in the calculation of teacher load. Specific means of computing load will be described in detail in the chapters discussing elementary and secondary school instructional programming techniques, but some general principles will be reviewed at this time.

To some principals, teacher load is indicated by the single factor of *pupil-teacher ratio* computed either on a daily basis in the elementary school or on a total average basis in the secondary schools. One problem with this simplified version of load is that the pupil-teacher ratio may be computed differently by the central office than by the attendance center personnel. The central office may include all nonteaching counselors, administrators, department or grade-level chairmen, and team leaders in their figures, thus producing a much lower ratio. School district officials may correctly report a pupil-staff ratio of twenty-five—one, but many teachers may have thirty-five pupils in a classroom. The teacher-pupil ratio should *not* be confused with the *staff-pupil ratio,* for the former ratio is a better indicator of the true teacher load.

Bent and McCann list the following major elements which

directly affect teachers work load (Parentheses indicate the writer's additions):

1. Total number of class sections (or sessions in elementary) per week.
2. The average number of pupils per class.
3. The subject (subjects in elementary) taught.
4. Number of preparations per day.
5. The pupil activities sponsored.
6. Teacher participation in the administration of the school.
7. Participation in professional activities.
8. Sociological climate of the particular school.[4]

To this list we might add the following:

9. Playground and lunchroom duty assignments.
10. Study hall or detention hall assignments.
11. Number of periods per day (secondary).

ADDITIONAL FACTORS AFFECTING SCHEDULING

Since numerous items must be considered by the individuals responsible for structuring the school schedule, the following additional factors are considered vital to the development of a sound, workable guide of operations.

1. Qualification and availability of teachers
2. Assignment of teachers
3. School transportation pattern
4. Buildings and facilities
5. Finance
6. Extra class activities
7. Lunch
8. Homeroom or advisory positions
9. Minimum days and make-up days
10. Assemblies, field days, etc.
11. Method of registration
12. State laws
13. Federal programs
14. Availability of data processing or related "hardware"

---

[4]Rudyard K. Bent and Lloyd E. McCann, p. 217.

There are countless progeny of the items discussed in this chapter and an *awareness* of them is of utmost importance to the scheduling technician. All elements are common to all schools regardless of grade level; however, the emphasis varies with the locale and the philosophy of education in that locale.

QUESTIONS AND SUGGESTIONS FOR STUDY

1. Research indicates that the class size is reportedly becoming smaller, yet teaching loads have been increasing. Explain.

2. Using the factors listed in this chapter to be considered in calculating teacher load, design a checklist to review the teacher-load pattern in your school and nearby schools. What factors were considered? Was there a difference between the elementary and secondary schools? How can this be explained?

3. Interview several elementary, junior high, and senior high principals to determine what general factors are considered before construction of the schedule begins. What items can you add to the list in this chapter?

4. Visit a school or district using a computer to schedule classes. What factors do they consider in preparing a schedule? How do these factors differ from the elements discussed in this chapter?

SELECTED REFERENCES

Austin, David B.; French, Will; and Hull, J. Dan. *American High School Administration,* 3rd ed. New York: Holt, Rinehart and Winston, 1962, Chapter 12, "Schedule-Making and School Organization."

Bent, Rudyard K., and McCann, Lloyd E. *Administration of Secondary Schools.* New York: McGraw-Hill, 1960, Chapter 12, "Coordinating the School Program."

Bush, Robert N. "Decision for the Principal: Hand or Computer Scheduling?" *Bulletin of the NASSP* 48 (April 1964): 141-46.

Glogau, Lillian, and Fessel, Murrary. *The Nongraded Primary School.* West Nyack, New York: Parker Publishing Co., 1967.

Goodlad, John I., and Anderson, Robert H. *The Nongraded Elementary School,* rev. ed. New York: Harcourt, Brace, and World, 1963.

Jacobson, Paul B.; Reavis, William C.; and Logsdon, James D. *The Effective School Principal,* 2d ed. Englewood Cliffs, New Jersey: Prentice-Hall, 1963, Chapters 3 and 4, "Planning the Year's Work" and "Making a School Schedule."

Linder, Ivan H., and Gunn, Henry M. *Secondary School Administration: Problems and Practices.* Charles E. Merrill Publishing Co., 1963, Chapter 11, "Schedule Construction and Registration."

Ovard, Glen F. *Administration of the Changing Secondary School.* New York: Macmillan, 1966, Chapters 7 and 8, "Schedule-Making and Organization" and "Organization, Administration, and Utilization of the Staff."

Chapter Two

Registration: Procedures Governing the Learner's Entry into Elementary and Secondary School Opportunities

Before the working pattern of instructional activities can be completed, students must be admitted and registered for classes through some procedure established by the school. Except for unique or special programs, registration procedures governing the entry of learners at the elementary level is simpler than at the secondary level. The roster of students is available from the previous teacher, and these records simply are transferred to the next level of grade, while transfer students, kindergarten, and new first grade students generally are required to register individually with the parents present.

Registration on the secondary level, or in any departmentalized plan whether secondary or elementary, involves the integration of state requirements, student selections, teacher qualifications, units of time, and subject offerings into a comprehensive, understandable chart of operations. How this one phase of managerial responsibility is handled usually is the key factor for determining whether the school year begins in a calm, businesslike fashion or in complete chaos.

Preregistration has become a vital factor in effective school operation. Regardless of the size of the school or the grade level, the planning of registration procedures for the next school year should be started in February or March with plans completed no later than the middle of May. Preferably, these plans should be concluded earlier than May. By this time any special tests should have been administered and test results data made available for use in registering students.

Three weeks is a maximum amount of time that should be required for preregistration procedures, although two weeks generally provides adequate time. The range of educational opportunities should be made known to students, time for counseling students and parents should be provided, and the actual registration procedures involving students should be accomplished within this period of time.

There are several major advantages to a spring preregistration period.

1. Preregistration helps to determine faculty needs for the coming year. Consequently, the earlier in the spring preregistration takes place the more accurate will be the estimated need for new faculty.
2. Space needs can be determined early. Even though it requires nearly two years to complete new buildings, temporary facilities and extended or double sessions can be anticipated.
3. Equipment and books can be ordered during the summer.
4. Budget estimates can be made more accurately.
5. Library, transportation, cafeteria, and related services can be planned more efficiently.
6. Schedules can be studied and revised during the time periods of less pressure of the summer.
7. Meaningful instruction can begin with the business of teaching and learning on the first school day. Since only students who have not preregistered will need to register in the fall, such registration can be arranged to take place in the evenings or on Saturdays before the new school year begins.
8. If the school has a mid-year promotion and graduation policy, preregistration can provide the necessary continuity of programs for the students and the school.

REGISTRATION IN THE ELEMENTARY SCHOOL

Before actual registration procedures are adapted, the type of curricular offerings should be designed. Otto and Sanders have defined three basic types of course offerings for consideration at the elementary level. Because these types are determined and controlled somewhat by state requirements, they vary considerably among the states.

Determining Curricular Offerings.   Otto and Sanders have identified the first pattern of offerings as a "subjects-taught-in-isolation" type of curriculum. A graphic example is portrayed in Figure 2.1.

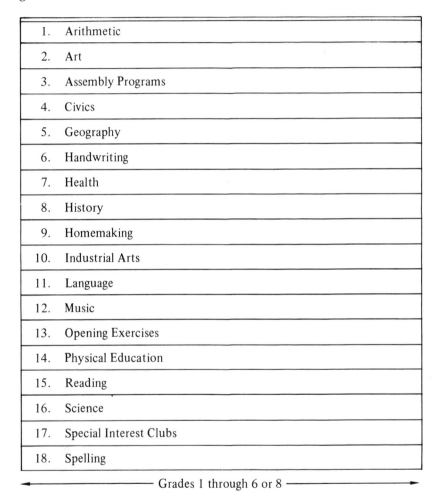

1.	Arithmetic
2.	Art
3.	Assembly Programs
4.	Civics
5.	Geography
6.	Handwriting
7.	Health
8.	History
9.	Homemaking
10.	Industrial Arts
11.	Language
12.	Music
13.	Opening Exercises
14.	Physical Education
15.	Reading
16.	Science
17.	Special Interest Clubs
18.	Spelling

⟵————————— Grades 1 through 6 or 8 —————————⟶

FIGURE 2.1. Subjects-Taught-in-Isolation Type of Curriculum[1]

[1]Henry J. Otto and David C. Sanders, *Elementary School Organization and Administration,* 4th ed. (New York: Appleton-Century-Crofts, 1964), p. 49. Copyright © 1964 by Meredith Publishing Company. Reprinted by permission of Appleton-Century-Crofts, Educational Division, Meredith Corporation.

Figure 2.2 portrays one pattern for a *core curriculum.*

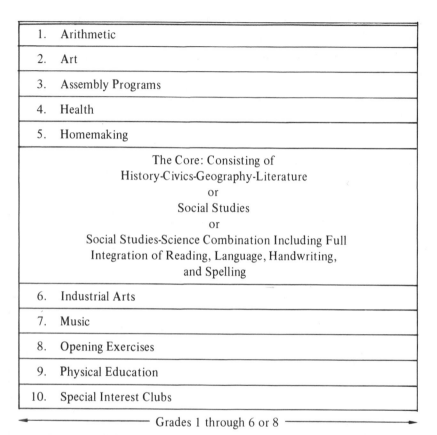

1.	Arithmetic
2.	Art
3.	Assembly Programs
4.	Health
5.	Homemaking

The Core: Consisting of
History-Civics-Geography-Literature
or
Social Studies
or
Social Studies-Science Combination Including Full
Integration of Reading, Language, Handwriting,
and Spelling

6.	Industrial Arts
7.	Music
8.	Opening Exercises
9.	Physical Education
10.	Special Interest Clubs

◄──────────── Grades 1 through 6 or 8 ────────────►

FIGURE 2.2. Core Curriculum Offerings in the Elementary School[2]

Figure 2.3 depicts the *broad fields curriculum* design for elementary schools as described by the same author.

A column might be added to the right of Figures 2, 3, or 4 to list the number of minutes each class meets on a daily or weekly basis. Thus, the state requirements in total minutes per day, week, half-year, or year would be available for information to the teacher, the counselor, the parent, and for state records. In-

---

[2]Otto and Sanders, p. 51.

Language Arts	
Social Studies	
Arithmetic	
Science and Health	
Physical Education	Creative
Music	and Recreative
Art and Handicraft	Arts

←——————————— Grades 1 through 6 or 8 ——————————→

FIGURE 2.3. Broad Fields Curriculum Design for Elementary Schools[3]

novative programs could also be planned around these basic requirements.

A study conducted for the U.S. Office of Education by Stuart E. Dean in 1959 reported in 1960 that there was some likelihood of increasing the length of the school day to meet the demands

Hours	Grades 1-3	Grades 4-6	Grades 7-8
4-4½	12.0	.8	.8
5	29.5	14.0	6.3
5½	40.9	45.4	37.1
6	14.5	36.5	46.0
Other	2.6	2.2	6.3
No answer	.5	1.1	3.5
Total	100.0	100.0	100.0

FIGURE 2.4. Number of Hours in the Elementary School Day, Exclusive of Lunch Period, by U.S. Percentages[4]

[3]Otto and Sanders, p. 52.

[4]Stuart E. Dean, *Elementary School Administration and Organization*, Bulletin 60, number 11 (Washington, D.C.: U.S. Office of Education, U.S. Department of Health, Education and Welfare, 1960), pp. 35-36.

of an expanding curriculum. Figure 2.4 provides data adapted from this study.

The matter of time should be considered carefully before proceeding with student registration, as it may control what course offerings are planned and the emphasis to be placed on the type of curricular design considered.

Stoddard has suggested that elementary schools divide their programs into two parts. One category, the *cultural imperatives* (language arts, social science, physical education), would include skills and knowledge essential to everyone, with students following a graded plan in a traditional structure. Stoddard has described the second category as *cultural electives* (mathematics, science, music, art, foreign language) which would be nongraded and allow students to move upward through each subject at their own rate.[5]

These plans and other organizational devices, such as nongrading, semi-departmentalization, platoons, and team teaching, affect and control both registration and scheduling procedures at the elementary level. It is imperative that all concerned understand the organization of the programs before registration and scheduling activities begin.

Registration Forms and Procedures.   Illustrated in Figure 2.5 is a sample of the student registration form used in an elementary school of approximately 800 students. The same card serves as an enrollment form for kindergarten and first grade. Information from these cards, plus the data entered on the new cumulative record folder, is tabulated and summarized in various ways to determine student placement and schedules. Again, the organizational pattern and the system of curricular offerings depends upon the established school policy.

Normally, the list of students assigned to self-contained classrooms is simply forwarded to the next grade level for the coming school year. In the spring, the teachers are asked to check the students on the list who will be passing and failing, and the students passing are transferred to the next grade as a group. Exceptions are made through either parental or teacher re-

---

[5]George D. Stoddard, *The Dual Progress Plan* (New York: Harper and Row Publishers, 1961).

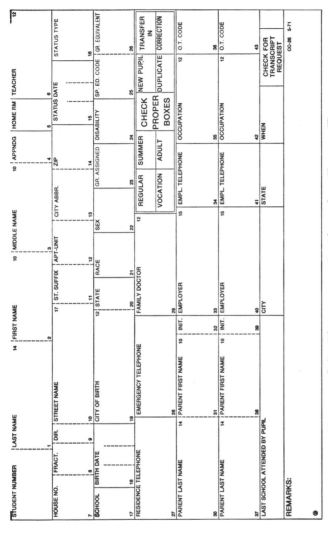

FIGURE 2.5. Elementary Registration Form. (Reproduced by courtesy of Clark County School District, Las Vegas, Nevada.)[6]

[6]This form and all materials used in the Clark County School District are reproduced through the courtesy of Kenny C. Guinn, Superintendent of Schools, Las Vegas, Nevada.

quests. Adjustments are also made for those not passing. A sample placement card is illustrated in Figure 2.6.

Student's Name_____ Grade_____

Subject_____ Teacher_____

Present Placement_____Recommended Placement_____

Justification for this recommendation:

FIGURE 2.6. Individual Student Preregistration Placement Card. (Reproduced by courtesy of Laura Dearing Elementary School, Clark County School District, Las Vegas, Nevada.)

Several schools ask secretaries to report early in the fall and phone each parent to ascertain whether or not his children will be in attendance during the coming school year. Adjustments for dropouts, migrants, and new students are then made, the lists revised, and classrooms assigned.

If nongraded or grouping plans are used, the data pertaining to each student is recorded on individual cards. During the spring, teachers discuss the children and locate them into phases, levels, or groups by sorting the cards. A second check on enrollment is then made in the fall. Figure 2.7 illustrates a card used to preregister and place students by reading ability.

REGISTRATION IN THE SECONDARY SCHOOL

As was indicated earlier, the practice of preregistration has become quite commonplace in schools today; registration per se has become a final check on the total school operation just before school opens. As a consequence, the principles and

Student's Name_____ Teacher_____

Grade_____ Recommended Reading Placement for 1968-1969_____

Reading_____ Student Ability   H HA A LA L
       (May 29th)

Pertinent Comments:

For office use only

Assignment for 68-69

Grade_____

Teacher_____

Room_____

Justification for change in reading placement: Reading Level_____

FIGURE 2.7. Elementary Level Preregistration Assignment Card. (Reproduced by courtesy of Laura Dearing School, Clark County School District, Las Vegas, Nevada.)

guidelines discussed in the following portion of this chapter will refer to both phases under the term *registration,* except when focusing upon a specific program or suggestion.

Careful planning is required before registration procedures are developed. Joint faculty-administrative committees should meet to determine the policies discussed in this chapter. Results of research conducted concerning the particular school's program should be disseminated to all faculty. Orientation seminars explaining new programs or the current program should be held for all students, interested parents, and faculty. Only then should the actual registration materials be worked out and the machinery set in motion.

One fact cannot be emphasized enough; the distribution of information and its understanding is of vital importance to the success of a registration program.

Registration Handbooks and Guides.   In the average or small-sized secondary school (600 students or fewer), the normal procedure for registration is usually as follows:

1. Students meet in advisory, homerooms, or counseling groups to study the registration handbook or list of course offerings.
2. Each student completes a registration sheet or registration cards, fills out other necessary forms, and turns in all information to the advisory or homeroom teacher.
3. Selected courses are then tallied and the schedule is constructed.

A key factor affecting the efficiency of this procedure is the packet containing registration information and instructions. These instructions generally are contained in registration sheets or some type of pamphlet or booklet. The expense of printing these booklets can be defrayed by charging the student a modest fee. However, no student should be deprived of instructions because of financial difficulty.

Some booklets or pamphlets are combination of student handbook, course catalog, and registration information. The organization of information in any booklet should be designed by the individual school to meet its specific needs. An outline of information related to the registration process which might be included in such a pamphlet follows:

1. *Table of Contents.* If the booklet's length is over three or four pages, a table of contents should be included. Even with fewer pages, an outline of the contents is often quite helpful to students, parents, and faculty in locating necessary information.
2. *Preface.* A preface explains the philosophy of the school. An outline of the program, if it differs from the traditional course of study, should be included in the preface. The following preface is taken from a course catalog for senior high students at Western High School, in the Clark County School District of Las Vegas, Nevada, and provides a sample of the type of information which might be included.

The emphasis at Western is upon the individual—our goal is "superior education individualized to the needs of each student." This is in contrast to a school which provided a program primarily for groups of students such as sophomores, juniors, seniors, college-bound, non-college-bound, fast, average, slow, etc.

The curriculum is nongraded to provide *appropriate placement.* This means that courses and procedures are organized to allow each student to be in just the "right educational place at the right time." With few exceptions, each semester a student may enroll in any course offered regardless of "grade" or year in school (the Course Catalog contains over 200 titles). In addition, within courses students may select the achievement level most suitable to them, ranging from Phase 1 to Phase 5.

Providing the right educational place for each student is important; however, encouraging and allowing each student to progress at his own best rate is also important. We have chosen to call this idea *continuous progress.* Even within a special course and phase, students still have widely differing interests, needs, and abilities. Our continuous progress strategies acknowledge these individual differences and attempt to utilize them to move each student as far as possible in a given length of time, regardless of the mythical "class average."

Since we have semester courses rather than year-long courses, students have the opportunity to select courses of their own individual preference each semester. It is vitally important that each student plan as early as possible his total high school program, based on his personal career needs, and then each semester select carefully those courses which provide the best sequence. Course selection is strictly a *student responsibility,* including the satisfaction of all graduation requirements. The information given throughout the Course Catalog is meant to assist the student in planning his high school program. Further assistance is available from teachers, counselors, administrators, and career and college publications in the library.[7]

---

[7]Theron Swainston, Principal, *Western High School Student Handbook* (Las Vegas, Nevada: Clark County School District, preface). Reprinted by permission of the author.

3. *Graduation Requirements.* State and local graduation requirements should be outlined with specific courses and credits (units) listed year by year. Note the following example adapted from the *Registration Guide* of Valley High School in the Clark County School District, Las Vegas, Nevada.

Registration Requirements

I. Each sophomore must select a course of study totaling at least 5 and not more than 5½ credits. Juniors and seniors must enroll for at least 5 and not more than 6 credits.

II. Each sophomore student must select a course of study that includes:
   A. English
   B. P.E. and Driver Education
   C. Health
   D. Classes in at least three of the following five areas (no more than one class in each area):
      1. Foreign Language
      2. Math
      3. Science
      4. Social Studies
      5. Business, Home Economics, Industrial Arts, Visual Arts, Music and Speech/Drama.

III. Each junior will be required to enroll in:
   A. English
   B. U.S. History
   C. Physical Education
   D. Appropriate electives. Consideration should be given to Educational/Vocational goals and graduation requirements.

IV. Each senior will be required to enroll in:
   A. English
   B. American Government
   C. Any courses required to make-up graduation deficiencies.
   D. Electives

NOTE: Students on the Selected Senior Program must: 1. maintain a 3.0 grade point average; 2. meet all graduation requirements; 3. have recommendation of counselor; and 4. be concurrently enrolled in a minimum of 4 credits at the high school level.[8]

4. *Special Program Requirements.* For example, enrollment information regarding county unit or multiple county vocational schools should be included.
5. *Maximum and Minimum Class Load.*
6. *Special Program Information.* On occasion courses may be organized by special groups or tracks. This is illustrated by the following:

Track B

The student who wishes to work in Track B must make a selection from the following courses:

English BI: English and Modern American Literature Credit 1.0
This course will consist of surveys of English and Modern American Literature with ample opportunity for analysis and commentary through composition.

English B2: Modern American Literature and Modern Media   Credit 1.0
During the first semester the student will survey Modern American Literature from 1860 to 1950. The second semester will involve examination analysis, and commentary upon modern communication media including newspapers, periodicals, television, etc.

Track C

Students who elect to work in Track C must make a selection from the following:

English CI: Practical Writing/Contemporary Reading Credit 1.0

---

[8]*Registration Guide* (Valley High School, Clark County School District, Las Vegas, Nevada 1968), p. 1. Reproduced by courtesy of Kenny C. Guinn, Superintendent of Schools, Las Vegas, Nevada.

High School Courses
(Grades 9-12)

(R) Required

Subject Title	Units	Grade
(R) 1. *Communicative Skills*		
(R) a. Language Arts:	4	
(R) Language Arts I	1	9
(R) Language Arts II	1	10
(R) Language Arts III	1	11
Language Arts IVA	1	12
Language Arts IVB	1	10-12
Grammar/Public Speaking	(½ each)	9
Fundamentals of Speech	1	10-12
Debate	1	9-12
Dramatics	1	9-12
b. Foreign Language		
Spanish I	1	9-11
Spanish II	1	10-12
Spanish III	1	11-12
(T) Latin I or French I	1	9-11
(T) Latin II	1	10-12

Subject Title	Units	Grade
(R) 6. Practical Arts		
a. Agriculture Education I	1	9
General Agriculture I	1	9
General Agriculture II	1	10
Advanced Agriculture	2	11-12
b. Business Education		
Basic Business Practices	1	10
Bookkeeping	1	11-12
Business Law/Economics	(½ each)	11-12
Secretary Practice I	1	12
Secretary Practice II	1	12
Typing	½ or 1	10-12
c. Homemaking		
Vocational Homemaking I	1	9-10
Vocational Homemaking II	1	10-11
Vocational Homemaking III	1	11-12

FIGURE 2.8. Course Listing for Registration

The student will study basic principles or writing expository prose, such as letters, reports, job resumes, etc. Emphasis will be placed on fundamentals of standard English usage and diction. In addition the student will read and discuss various literary selections with the intent of reading for message and pleasure. The goal will be increased enjoyment and understanding of the media.[9]

7. *Course Listings* by grade or subject area levels with brief course descriptions should be included. A variety of methods are used to present course information to the students. One example is the format used in item 6 of this list for the special course description. Another technique is to list subjects by departments or areas but to not include course descriptions. Students can refer to this sheet while registering. The course descriptions, if written at all, are included in either the student handbook or a separate document. An illustration of this format appears in Figure 2.8.

Students may plan all courses they intend to take during their high school years and record these on a plan sheet printed on the back of the registration schedule or attached as a separate sheet. Figure 2.9 illustrates one portion of a planning sheet.

8. *Directions for Registration.* Often, school officials will redistribute a set of instructions during the registration period to be certain that this information is available. A sample of the first page of a three-page instruction sheet utilized at Western High School in Las Vegas, Nevada, follows. The second and third pages, which are not included, continue to identify student procedures step by step in a unique college-style registration.

Spring Semester Registration - 1968

Instructions for Students

Things to do to Prepare for Registration

1. By studying the "Master Schedule" and the copy of your preregistration card, determine when you can get

---

[9]Ibid., p. 4.

Grade 12				
Subjects	Units	Changes	Date	Reason for Changes

Advisor's Comments:

Signed_____
(Advisor)

Signed_____
(Parent)

FIGURE 2.9. Portion of a Student Planning Sheet

the classes you have filled out as major or alternate selections on the side of the yellow registration card marked "Preregistration." *Do not, in any way, alter those course selections, or phase selections, since an altered card will prevent your enrolling.* If you must change your course selections, or phase selections, disregard your appointed registration time and report for registration on Monday, January 22, at 2:30 P.M.

2. When you are sure of the class schedule you want, fill in part A of the "Student's Copy of Program." (Part B of the "Student's Copy of Program" cannot be filled out until after you have enrolled in all your classes on registration day. Teachers will fill out the "Registration" side of the yellow card.)

3. If you have not preregistered, you should preregister and register with a counselor at 2:30 P.M. on January 22.

4. If a parent wants to change the "preregistration" course selections, or phases, he may do so; however, if the course selections, *or phases,* are changed, please disregard your registration appointment time and register on January 22 at 2:30 P.M. with the counselors in the Little Theater.

5. Be sure that you are properly groomed and that you wear proper school attire on registration day.

Registration Procedures

Step 1. If your registration card has not been in any way changed and it is your registration appointment time, report to the front (north) entrance of the school properly groomed and in proper school dress. Bring all your registration materials with you. (If you changed course and/or phase selections, report to the counselors in the Little Theater on January 22, at *2:30 P.M.*)

9. *A Registration Checklist.* This list assists in preventing the errors of omission that students make. Figure 2.10 illustrates one form of registration checklist used in the Clark County School District.

Name _____   Grade _____
    Last   First   M.   REGISTRATION CHECK LIST

1. CC-26 completed   _____

2. Attendance card information completed   _____

3. Locker card information completed   _____

4. ID Card   _____

5. Student schedule   _____

6. Senior Diploma Card completed   _____

FIGURE 2.10. Registration Check List. (Reproduced by courtesy of Clark County School District, Las Vegas, Nevada.)

A number of school principals also distribute question-and-answer sheets or booklets explaining the various programs, registration, and scheduling procedures. These are valuable public relations devices as well as sources of helpful information. Other administrators have developed a series of information booklets describing their curriculum, course of study, services, scheduling, and registration procedures.

Preregistration.   To illustrate the diversity that still exists in our secondary schools today, three different types of preregistration procedures are outlined and illustrated in the following pages. Schools from the Clark County District have been selected because individual schools in the district practice these different procedures. Variations and adaptations of these practices prevail throughout the county.

1. Preregistration or registration based on conventional curricular programs
2. Preregistration based on a computerized schedule using modules and a team-teaching organization involving large group, small group, and independent study
3. A college-type preregistration plan involving a totally nongraded program

A Conventional Program.   Preregistration in a conventional program generally occurs in early spring, preferably before April, and employs the following procedure:

1. Registration guides or sheets are distributed to all students in homerooms or advisories.
2. These materials are taken home, studied, and discussed with the parents; a trial or worksheet in the booklet may be partially worked out with the parents. A third or fourth year plan is generally developed.
3. In an extended advisory period, all students complete their pattern of courses (or educational experiences) on a schedule card using the course guides received earlier. Students often are asked to indicate alternative, or first and second priority, courses as electives in case a given course is not being offered or because the time it is offered conflicts with a higher priority study interest. This card or a copy is mailed or forwarded to the home for the parent's signature. Even though this may appear to be a time-consuming process, the involvement of parents early in the planning process generally prevents later frustrations and time-consuming adjustments.

   The preregistration cards are often *color coded* (e.g., green for sophomores, yellow for juniors, white for seniors) to facilitate identification. Key-sort punch cards may be utilized to speed up the alphabetizing, sorting, and scheduling processes. This mechanical approach may be superseded by optical scanning or punched card input systems for computer-based data processing approaches.

As a matter of procedure, seniors are given registration priority. They may soon be terminating their tenure in school and home; possible conflicts may delay satisfaction of graduation requirements.

4. The completed registration cards provide data essential to the preparation of the *master schedule.* In some schools, master schedules developed in prior years may be used to provide the course selection information which students need for preregistration or registration in subsequent years. In such cases, the student makes his plans as though the schedule presented were applicable during the registration period. This procedure may be acceptable in large and stable attendance centers. The Master Schedule will of necessity be revised at least every second year to meet the changing needs of students as revealed in their preregistration information. New students generally are registered individually as they move into the community.

Registration of Feeder Students. A particularly important phase of the preregistration or registration procedure is the orientation of students from the elementary or junior high feeder schools. The junior high school generally receives the bulk of its students from the sixth grade or from one of the higher elementary grades, depending upon the district organizational pattern. High schools usually acquire students from another secondary system, normally the junior high, although four-year high schools receive their "feeder" students from the eighth grade.

Regardless of the source, an orientation and preregistration system should be developed. Linder and Gunn have developed a flow chart which describes the steps that might be taken in programming students from feeder schools into the junior/senior high program (see Figure 2.11).

Normally, the guidance personnel work quite closely with both parents and students from feeder schools. In many instances, evening homeroom sessions are held for both parents

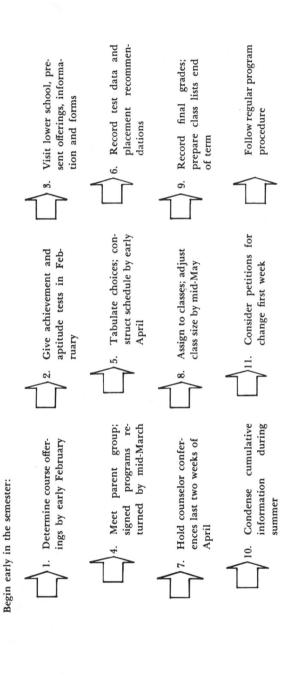

Begin early in the semester:

1. Determine course offerings by early February

2. Give achievement and aptitude tests in February

3. Visit lower school, present offerings, information and forms

4. Meet parent group; signed programs returned by mid-March

5. Tabulate choices; construct schedule by early April

6. Record test data and placement recommendations

7. Hold counselor conferences last two weeks of April

8. Assign to classes; adjust class size by mid-May

9. Record final grades; prepare class lists end of term

10. Condense cumulative information during summer

11. Consider petitions for change first week

Follow regular program procedure

FIGURE 2.11. A Flow Chart For Transitional Guidance. (Steps in the preparation and programming of 8th graders entering a four-year high school or 9th graders a three-year school.)[10]

[10]Ivan H. Linder and Henry M. Gunn, *Secondary School Administration: Problems and Practices* (Columbus, Ohio: Charles E. Merrill Publishing Co., 1963), p. 176. Copyright © 1963 by Charles E. Merrill Publishing Co. Reprinted by permission of the publisher.

and pupils to assist with preregistration procedures. High school students provide invaluable assistance with orientation and actual registration for classes.

Registration in the Junior High or Middle School.   Although a majority of junior high or middle schools are departmentalized, curricular offerings often are varied enough to warrant special attention and modification of procedures found at the senior high school. As was stated earlier, the organization of the curriculum does affect registration plans and procedures.

A survey by Grace S. Wright indicates that the block-time core program class schedules are the most prevalent curricular organization utilized at this level. Figure 2.12 illustrates the results of this survey.

Enrollment	Number of Schools Returning Questionnaire	Schools Reporting Block-Time Classes	
		Number	Per Cent
All schools	2517	487	19.3
Less than 200	1185	83	7.0
200 to 400	704	131	18.5
500 to 999	425	165	40.0
1,000 and over	203	108	50.3

FIGURE 2.12. Number and Per Cent of Schools Having Block-Time Classes[11]

More recent studies by individuals consistently support this data. The "core" concept simplifies registration in the junior high school because students have fewer electives and the required courses are blocked into groups of subjects.

The procedures for registration generally follow the pattern utilized by senior high schools. Because the Master Schedule is

---

[11]Grace S. Wright, *Block-Time Classes and the Core Program in the Junior High School,* U.S. Office of Education Bulletin No. 6 (Washington, D.C.: Government Printing Office, 1958), Table 3, p. 6.

frequently based on the *block* or *group* plan, registration can usually be conducted by using simplified forms and key-sort cards. Computers are used in instances where such equipment is available; in these cases, the same pattern of registration is followed as that reported earlier in this chapter. Figure 2.13 illustrates a typical registration information sheet for a large junior high school in the Clark County School System.

The following are the requirements for Eighth-Grade Students at Von Tobel Junior High:

1. Social Studies (American History)
2. English
3. Math
4. Science
5. Physical Education

To complete your schedule of 7 classes, you must pick 3 electives in order of preference. Resource Centers are available only where schedule conflicts occur.

Art	Girl's Glee Club
Home Economics	Boy's Glee Club
Typing	Beginner Band
Wood Shop	Intermediate Band
Craft	Varsity Band
Spanish I	Communications
French I	

FIGURE 2.13. A Partial List of Requirements. (Reproduced by courtesy of Von Tobel Junior High School, Clark County School District, Las Vegas, Nevada.)

Figure 2.14 illustrates a partial list of course offerings and code numbers for the eighth grade. Normally, all these grade level curricula are printed on one long sheet to assist the students in planning all three years of the junior high program. The term *Resource Center* refers to independent study areas for the students.

Grade 8			
Code Number	Course Title	Code Number	Course Title
101	English 8	900	Typing
201	Math 8	801	Wood Shop
202	Algebra 8	908	Boy's Physical Education
301	History 8	103	Communications
401	Science 8	405	Resource Center
601	Art 8		
606	Home Economics 8		

FIGURE 2.14. Partial List of Course Offerings. (Reproduced by courtesy of Von Tobel Junior High School, Clark County School District, Las Vegas, Nevada.)

Figures 2.15 and 2.16 depict the front and back preregistration and registration card used by each student at Von Tobel Junior High School.

Preregistration information is collected during the spring so that the Master Schedule can be constructed. When the student registers in the fall, he uses the Master Schedule as his final reference.

If a computer is used at either the junior or senior high school level, the students generally do not have a choice of instructor. However, the choice of instructor is of less importance in those schools when team-teaching is involved, since the student works with a complete team of professionals and paraprofessionals rather than with a single instructor.

It is of vital importance that a strong orientation system be developed to provide preregistration and registration assistance for the feeder elementary schools. A successful spring preregistration program can set the tone for a positive attitude toward secondary education and provide the needed motivation to keep many youngsters in school when they reach the secondary level.

In recent years, the trend has been to include explanations of the curricular program, preregistration and registration proce-

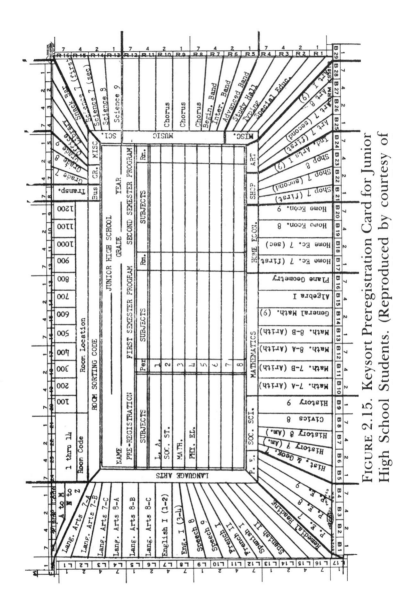

FIGURE 2.15. Keysort Preregistration Card for Junior High School Students. (Reproduced by courtesy of Von Tobel Junior High School, Clark County School District, Las Vegas, Nevada.)

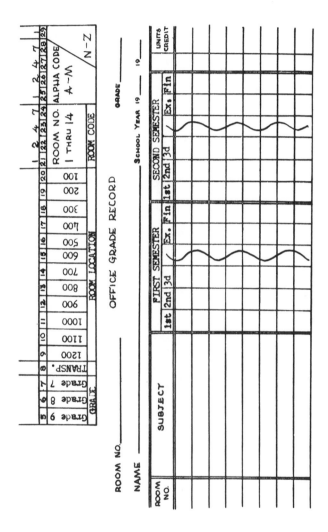

FIGURE 2.16. Keysort Registration Card for Junior High School Students. (Reproduced by courtesy of Von Tobel Junior High School, Clark County School District, Las Vegas, Nevada.)

39

dures, and course descriptions in a student handbook. This has been an important source of information for the use of both parents and students in understanding and planning the student's junior and senior high school program. Districts operating with the middle-school plan which utilizes a departmentalized core program for Grades 5-8 should adopt the same procedures. Consequently, it is recommended that the items pertaining to registration be included in the student handbook. The values that can result from providing this information should outweigh any additional time or cost involved in including these materials.

QUESTIONS AND SUGGESTIONS FOR STUDY

1. What are the values of preregistration?

2. Why should the type of curricular program and its organization be determined before registration procedures are outlined?

3. What preliminary data must be accumulated before actual schedule construction can take place?

4. Study the preregistration and registration of the elementary, middle school or junior high, and senior high schools in your area and describe their differences.

5. Develop a sample student handbook, including a set of preregistration and registration instructions, a sample of the various forms to be used, and a catalog description of the subjects offered.

SELECTED REFERENCES

Anderson, Lester W., and Van Dyke, Lauren A. *Secondary School Administration*. Boston: Houghton Mifflin, 1963, Chapter 6, "Organization of the School Schedule and Calendar."

Bossing, Nelson, and Cramer, Roscoe V. *The Junior High School.* Boston: Houghton Mifflin, 1965, Chapters 6 and 7, "Block-Time Class Organization" and "The Core Curriculum."

Brown, B. Frank. *The Nongraded High School.* Englewood Cliffs, New Jersey: Prentice-Hall, 1963, Chapter 6, "Making the Curriculum Meaningful to Students."

Dufay, Frank R. *Ungrading the Elementary School.* West Nyack, New York: Parker Publishing Co., 1966, Chapter 2, "Grouping: The Vital Preliminary."

Jacobson, Paul B.; Reavis, William C.; and Logsdon, James D. *The Effective School Principal,* 2d ed. Englewood Cliffs, New Jersey: Prentice-Hall, 1963, Chapter 4, "Making a School Schedule."

Linder, Ivan H., and Gunn, Henry M. *Secondary School Administration: Problems and Practices.* Columbus, Ohio: Charles E. Merrill Publishing Co., Chapter 11, "Schedule Construction and Registration."

Manlove, Donald C., and Beggs, David W. III. *Flexible Scheduling.* Bloomington: University of Indiana Press, 1966.

Otto, Henry J., and Sanders, David C. *Elementary School Organization and Administration,* 4th ed. New York: Appleton-Century-Crofts, 1964, Chapters 2 and 3, "Curriculum Issues" and "Organization for Instruction."

Ovard, Glen F. *Administration of the Changes in Secondary School.* New York: Macmillan, 1966, Chapters 6 and 7, "The Annual Cycle —Beginning and Ending the School Year" and "Schedule Making."

Wright, Grace S. *Block-Time Classes and the Core Program in the Junior High School.* U.S. Office of Education Bulletin Number 6. Washington, D.C.: Government Printing Office, 1958, Table 3, p. 6.

Chapter Three

The Master Schedule:
The Comprehensive
Programming Instrument

The Master Schedule is the comprehensive record of course offerings in an individual school attendance center. Designed to encompass those variables unique to each attendance unit, its development rests on the application of certain common principles.

Because of its comprehensive nature, the *Master Schedule* itself may not be distributed to all faculty and students, but it should be available in the principal's office for review or study at any time. Information from the Master Record is distributed to the students, however. During preregistration, for example, a schedule of courses identifying the subjects offered is often distributed to students for their personal use. Figure 3.1 illustrates this type of schedule. Note that the subject areas are clearly indicated in the left column.

After this information has been utilized for registration, the Master Schedule is constructed. The *teaching* or *class schedule* is then distributed to the faculty and students. Normally, this schedule lists the individual faculty member along either the top of the schedule or the left side. Larger secondary schools will then group faculty by departments or team areas. A sample *teaching schedule* adapted from a Master Schedule is depicted in Figure 3.2.

Period	1	2	3	4	5	6	7
Start Finish	8:00 8:55	9:00 9:55	10:00 11:00	(class) 11:05 - 12:00 11:05 - 11:45 (lunch)	(lunch) 12:05 - 12:45 11:50 - 12:45 (class)	12:50 1:45	1:50 2:45
American Government I	Miss E. Milton Phase 4-5 Room 310		Miss E. Milton Phase 2 Room 310				
	Mr. J. Holliday Phase 3 Room 121		Mr. J. Holliday Phase 3 Room 121				
American Government II	Mr. D. Billedeaux Phase 3 Room 124	Mr. K. Muster Phase 2 Room 119	Mr. D. Billedeaux Phase 3 Room 124	Mr. D. Billedeaux Phase 4-5 Room 124		Mr. K. Muster Phase 2 Room 119	
	Mr. K. Muster Phase 2 119	Mr. J. Holliday Phase 3 Room 121	Mr. K. Muster Phase 2 Room 119	Mr. K. Muster Phase 2 Room 119		Mr. R. Martinez Phase 3 Room 123	
	Mr. R. Martinez Phase 3 Room 123	Mr. R. Martinez Phase 4-5 Room 123	Mr. R. Martinez Phase 3 Room 123	Mr. J. Holliday Phase 3 Room 121			
	Mr. J. Cebular Phase 3 606						
U.S. History I			Mrs. B. Douglas Phase 3-5 Room 224			Mrs. B. Douglas Phase 2-3 Room 224	

FIGURE 3.1. Portion of Registration Schedule Emphasizing Subject Areas. (Reproduced by courtesy of Western High School, Clark County School District, Las Vegas, Nevada.)

CONSTRUCTING THE MASTER
SCHEDULE: SECONDARY

In addition to the normal items of information involved in the class and registration schedules, the Master Schedule should contain a comprehensive report of all factors related to the operation of the school. A brief outline of these factors follows.

1. Units of time, including beginning and ending of any given period or module, as well as the start and end of the school day and time between each period or module to facilitate movement of students
2. Course name, number, and description
3. Room numbers
4. Maximum and current enrollment in each class
5. Total enrollment per period to double check the schedule (e.g., if enrollment equals 400 students, but classes account for only 300 during a specific time period, where are the missing 100 students?)
6. Preparation or conference periods for staff
7. Special classes, blocking time, special education, etc.
8. Color code for classes that are specifically at one grade level or are of one ability group
9. Department areas
10. Lunch periods
11. Schedules for the following:

   a. Assembly
   b. Activity
   c. Minimum day
   d. Advisory or homeroom period, if such a period not scheduled daily
   e. Rotation, if rotation method is utilized

Figure 3.3 illustrates what a comprehensive Master Schedule might include.

Social Sciences							
42. Mr. D. Billedeaux	Am. Government II Phase 3, 124	Social Science IV Phase 3-5, 124	Am. Government II Phase 3, 124	Am. Government II Phase 4-5, 124	Lunch	Curriculum Development	Conference
43. Mr. H. Hawkins	Conference	Social Science IV Phase 3-5, 126	U.S. History II Phase 2, 126	U.S. History II Phase 3, 126	Lunch	Curriculum Development	U.S. History II Phase 4-5, 126
44. Miss N. Hargett	Conference	Social Science IV Phase 3-5, 125	U.S. History II Phase 3, 125	U.S. History II Phase 3, 125	Lunch	Curriculum Development	U.S. History II Phase 2, 125
45. Dr. R. Cremer	U.S. History II Phase 3, 226	U.S. History II Phase 2, 226	U.S. History II Phase 4-5, 226	Lunch	Ancient History Phase 4, 226	U.S. History II Phase 3, 226	Conference
46. Mrs. B. Douglas	U.S. History II Phase 4-5, 224	U.S. History II Phase 3, 224	U.S. History I Phase 3-5, 224	Conference	Lunch	U.S. History I Phase 2-3, 224	U.S. History II Phase 3, 224
47. Mr. K. Muster	Am. Government II Phase 2, 119	Am. Government II Phase 2, 119	Am. Government II Phase 2, 119	Am. Government II Phase 2, 119	Lunch	Am. Government II Phase 2, 119	Conference
48. Mr. J. Holliday	Am. Government I Phase 3, 121	Am. Government II Phase 3, 121	Am. Government II Phase 3, 121	Am. Government II Phase 3, 121	Lunch	Curriculum Development	Conference
49. Mr. R. Martinez	Am. Government II Phase 3, 123	Am. Government II Phase 4-5, 123	Am. Government II Phase 3, 123	Lunch	Current Affairs & Events, Phase 2-4, 123	Am. Government II Phase 3, 123	Conference
50. Mr. D. Davison	Psychology Phase 3-4, 117	Psychology Phase 3, 117	Conference	Psychology Phase 4, 117	Lunch	Psychology Phase 3, 117	Psychology Phase 3, 117
51. Mr. J. Brailsford	Conference	Sociology Phase 3-4, 220	Marriage and the Family, Phase 3, 220	Marriage and the Family, Phase 3, 220	Lunch	Marriage and the Family, Phase 3, 220	Sociology Phase 4, 220

FIGURE 3.2. Sample Teaching Schedule. (Reproduced by courtesy of Western High School, Clark County School District, Las Vegas, Nevada.)

Master Schedules may be constructed on large metallic boards which utilize small magnetic blocks to hold information in place or on pocket-type boards which permit information on slips or cards to be inserted into the pockets at certain points. Some principals prefer to use a large glass plate and felt marking materials similar to those used by television weather reporters to place necessary information at given points. Since new ideas will emerge during the scheduling process, the device used to place and enter the information must be flexible (i.e., the figures may be able to be erased or replaced in a relatively easy fashion in order to accommodate the necessary revisions).

CONSTRUCTING THE MASTER SCHEDULE: ELEMENTARY

The Master Schedule for the elementary school should contain the same basic information as that which was previously discussed under secondary school scheduling. This information may be very similar to that found in the secondary school where departmentalization occurs at the elementary school level. Differences will occur in the self-contained organizational pattern characteristic of the majority of elementary programs. Consequently, the principal may need to use the book-type display device shown in Figure 6.2 to enter all the necessary information in a room-by-room pattern. In smaller schools, principals have utilized large magnetic boards, a special blackboard, or glass plates to record the entire school schedule. Several schools post one-page copies of each teacher's class schedule on a large bulletin board. Special schedules for library, music, physical education, and art should also be entered on the Master Schedule.

The elementary school Master Schedule may be organized either by grade levels or by rooms; in schools with the campus plan, it may be plotted by buildings. Examples of the three types of composite Master Schedules are illustrated in Figures 3.4, 3.5 and 3.6.

Figure 3.7 illustrates a room and teacher's schedule, one unit of a composite Master Schedule. Figures 3.8 and 3.9 illustrate special library and music schedules in the same school.

High School
Master Schedule

Period	Time	Advisor Homeroom		1		2		3	
		8:00 8:10	ENR / CAP	8:15 9:10	ENR / CAP	9:15 10:15	ENR / CAP	10:15 11:00	ENR / CAP
English Miss A		10th A202	30 / 35	English 10A A202	27 / 35	English 10B A202	28 / 35	Preparation A202	27 / 35
Mr. B			30 / 35	Preparation A203	— / 35	English 10C A203	30 / 35	English 10C A203	28 / 35
Mrs. C		10th A204	25 / 30	English 11A A204	25 / 30	English 12B A204	20 / 30	French I B212	30 / 40
Mr. D		11th A205	30 / 35	English 11B A205	20 / 35	English 11B A205	25 / 35	English 11C A205	25 / 35
Mrs. E		12th A206	30 / 30	Journalism II B104	20 / 25	Journalism II B104	20 / 25	English 12A A206	20 / 30
Social Studies Mr. F		B212	30 / 30	U.S. History B212	30 / 30	Boys PE G11 MWF	70 / 80	Health G114 TTH PE G112 MWF	40 / 40
	Total			Total Enrollment		Total Enrollment		Total Enrollment	

(Total Enrolled = Total Students Each Period)

FIGURE 3.3. Sample Portion of a Master Schedule.

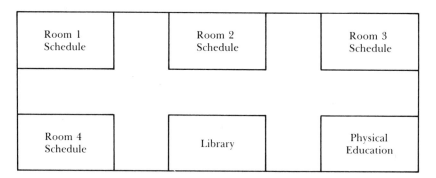

FIGURE 3.4. Elementary Master Schedule Board by Rooms.

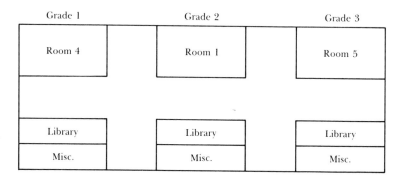

FIGURE 3.5. Elementary Master Schedule Board by Grade Levels.

Bldg. 100 Room 112 Grade 4		Bldg. 200 Room 214 Grade 5		Bldg. 300 Room 316 Grade 6
Library		Bldg. 400 Music Room 401		Bldg. 400 Art Room 402

FIGURE 3.6. Elementary Master Schedule Board by Buildings.

Room 4 – Teacher's Schedule

Time	Activity	
8:45	Assemble with homeroom on blacktop for flag ceremony	
8:50-9:00	Pupil-teacher Planning	
9:00-10:30	Reading, Physical Education, and Music	

	Monday-Tuesday-Wednesday-Thursday*	Friday

	Group	A	B	C	
9:00-9:30		R	PE	M	10:00-10:30
9:30-10:00		PE	M	R	10:30-11:00
10:00-10:30		M	R	PE	11:00-11:30

Time	Activity	
10:30-10:35	Break	Monday 10:30-10:55 Library Room 35
10:35-11:00	Science, Social Studies, Health, and Safety	Conference with Evans
11:00-11:20	Writing	Friday 9:00-9:55 Art Room 8
11:20-11:35	Spelling	Conference and/or Preparation
11:35-12:00	Arithmetic	
12:00-12:35	Lunch 12:35 Meet homeroom on blacktop and proceed to classroom	
12:40-12:55	Story time	
12:55-1:35	Reading-Phonics	
1:35-1:40	Break	
1:40-2:15	Reading-Phonics	
2:15-2:45	Language Arts activities	
2:45-2:55	Evaluation	
2:55-3:00	Cleanup	
3:00	Dismissal	

*(Library instead of Music on Thursday)

FIGURE 3.7. Sample Teacher's Daily Room Schedule. (Courtesy, Laura Dearing Elementary School, Clark County School District, Las Vegas, Nevada.)

Library	Monday	Tuesday	Wednesday	Thursday	Friday
9:00 to 9:25	Room 27	Room 26	Room 23	4-5-17	18-19-20-21
9:30 to 9:55	Room 28	Room 22	Room 25	4-5-17	18-19-20-21
10:00 to 10:25	Room 29	Room 24		4-5-17	18-19-20-21
10:30 to 10:55	Room 4	Room 19	Room 18	26-27-28-29	22-23-24-25
11:00 to 11:25	Room 5	Room 20		26-27-28-29	22-23-24-25
11:30 to 11:55	Room 21	Room 17		26-27-28-29	22-23-24-25
12:40 to 1:40	6-2	4-4	5-1	4-2	4-1
1:40 to 2:10					
2:10 to 3:10	6-1	6-3	5-3	5-2	4-3

FIGURE 3.8. Library Schedule. (Reproduced by courtesy of Laura Dearing School, Clark County School District, Las Vegas, Nevada.)

Music – p.m.	Monday	Tuesday	Wednesday	Thursday	Friday
12:40 to 1:10	(5-1) (5-2) (5-3)	(6-2) (5-1) (5-2) (5-3)	(6-2) (5-2)	(6-2) (5-1) (5-3)	(6-2) (5-1) (5-2) (5-3)
1:10 to 1:40	(5-1) (5-2) (5-3)	(6-2) (5-1) (5-2) (5-3)	(6-2) (5-2)	(6-2) (5-1) (5-3)	(6-2) (5-1) (5-2) (5-3)
1:40 to 2:10	(6-3) (5-1) (5-2) (5-3) (4-1) (4-2) (4-3)	(6-1) (6-2) (5-1) (5-3) (5-2) (4-1) (4-2) (4-3)	(6-1) (6-2) (6-3) (5-2) (4-1) (4-2) (4-3)	(6-1) (6-2) (6-3) (5-1) (5-3) (4-2) (4-3)	(6-1) (6-2) (6-3) (5-1) (5-2) (5-3) (4-1)
2:10 to 2:40	(6-3) (4-1) (4-2) (4-3)	(6-1) (4-1) (4-2) (4-3)	(6-1) (6-3) (4-1) (4-2) (4-3)	(6-1) (6-3) (4-2) (4-3)	(6-1) (6-3) (4-1)
2:40 to 3:10	(6-3) (4-1) (4-2) (4-3)	(6-1) (4-1) (4-2) (4-3)	(6-1) (6-3) (4-1) (4-2) (4-3)	(6-1) (6-3) (4-2) (4-3)	(6-1) (6-3) (4-1)

FIGURE 3.9. Special Music Schedule.(Reproduced by courtesy of Laura Dearing School, Clark County School District, Las Vegas, Nevada.)

THE BLOCK OR GROUP SCHEDULE

The conventional *block* or *group schedule* is commonly used to identify and place groups of students who are registering for the same subjects or combinations of subjects. Generally, the block-scheduling technique is used at the junior-high level where there are many required courses and few electives and in smaller high schools where a minimum of half of the program is required.[1] This method of scheduling is also utilized in those elementary schools offering a semi-departmentalized or "platoon" group scheduling procedure, except in cases where non-grading and/or team-teaching are also a part of the program.

Block scheduling requires two basic steps. First, determine the number of groups of pupils taking the same subject or combination of subjects; divide this number into the required number of sections. Each *block* or *group* is assigned to different periods during the day.

> Example: In the seventh grade, 112 students have registered for English, history, math, science, and Health and Physical Education. This forms four sections of 28 students each.

Second, arrange the classes into a schedule according to their *groups* or *blocks* as charted in Figure 3-10. In this example, the numbers under Groups 1 through 4 indicate the class period each group will meet. An elective class has been added to complete the student program.

In high schools where only a portion of the classes can be grouped, these classes would be calculated first in the same manner as that outlined above; then, the various electives would be scheduled by using the *mosaic method* of scheduling that is described later in this chapter.

The block schedule is also referred to as a means of "blocking" out one to three periods of time for students in a particular

---

[1]Paul B. Jacobson, William C. Reavis and James D. Logsden, *The Effective School Principal,* 2d ed. (Englewood Cliffs, N.J.: Prentice-Hall Inc., 1963), p. 66. Copyright © 1963 by Prentice-Hall, Inc. Paraphrased by permission of the publisher.

Class	Group 1	Group 2	Group 3	Group 4
English 7	1	2	3	4
History 7	4	5	6	7
Math 7	7	1	2	3
Science 7	2	3	4	5
Health and Physical Education	3	4	5	6
Elective	5	6	7	1

FIGURE 3.10. Sample Work Sheet for Block Scheduling.

core of subjects all of which are scheduled to be held in the same room with the same teacher. For example:

Teacher	Period 1	Period 2
X	50 minutes Group 1 English 7 Room 214	50 minutes Group 1 History 7 Room 214

FIGURE 3.11

In the illustration above, the students are "cored" in English and history and are scheduled to meet two periods per day with the same teacher in Room 214. This plan provides the teacher with a time flexibility that is of considerable value in determining how the teaching-learning process will take place.

Several studies have indicated that block-time scheduling in the junior high school occurs most frequently at the seventh-grade level and less often in the ninth grade. Grace Wright's 1958 study on block-time classes and core programs presents the typical data supporting this conclusion. The following information summarizes one portion of her report.[2]

---

[2]Grace S. Wright, *Block-Time Classes and the Core Program in the Junior High School,* U.S. Office of Education, Bulletin No. 6. (Washington: Government Printing Office, 1958), p. 6.

Grade	Number Schools	Per Cent
7	459	94
8	351	72
9	125	26[3]

It should be noted that the introduction of block-time scheduling does require considerable planning and experimentation. Bossing and Cramer provide illustrations of specific block-time experimental plans in their book *The Junior High School,* and list five benefits accrued from the application of block-time classes as they were formulated by the junior high school teachers of West Junior High School in Kansas City, Missouri.[3]

1. The elimination of the general study hall was considered a learning benefit since study separated from class guidance and instruction is not very effective for the junior high school student. Throughout the school, correlation and integration in curriculum instruction was advanced, thereby reducing fragmented learning and grade retardation.

2. Student conduct during class period changes and lunch periods was positively responsive to increased stability and continuity in the situational controls afforded by the block-time class schedules, which place more students and their teachers in the same place at the same time.

3. Guidance needs of ninth-grade students are more observable and effectively met by incorporating homeroom in block-time classes. This benefit seems of marked import since students at this grade level are frequently struggling with conflicting attitudes toward continued education in senior high school. The fact that some of them are not protected by a compulsory school attendance law adds to the significance of this guidance resource.

4. All block-time class teachers have the same regular class period open in each grade for cooperative curriculum planning,

---

[3]Nelson L. Bossing and Roscoe V. Cramer, *The Junior High School* (Boston: Houghton Mifflin Co., 1965), pp. 136-139.

consultation, team-teaching, and student-teacher conferences during the seven-hour school day. The opportunities
for teachers to utilize a broader arena of group learning activities within both school and community which serve to stimu-
late and supplement subject content are definitely enhanced.

5. The application of block-time classes in all three grades is
considered essential to prevent the multiple conflicts and
disadvantages inherent when two different kinds of administration, guidance, and instruction are carried within the
framework of one junior high school.[4]

THE MOSAIC METHOD

The student-centered method of schedule construction is often
termed the *mosaic method of scheduling.* The concept is based
upon the practice of having students register for courses first
and then arranging the subsequent registration data into a
mosaic pattern until the programming is completed in the form
of a schedule. Some educators label this type of schedule construction as a "trial-and-error" method, a label which is true in
part since pieces of information or instructional resources
within the mosaic (teacher, course, room, and time) are often
arbitrarily moved about to provide the most effective and flexible organizational pattern possible.

The schedule or programming board should be of such design that it permits the "moving about" of pieces of data within
the mosaic. Frequently, pocket-type or magnetic boards are
used as devices to complement this schedule-building process,
particularly since the use of blackboard and chalk can easily
result in error through the accidental erasure of valuable information. The general procedure used in preparing an outline of
instructional programming is to list the time (periods) along the
top or left margin of the board and the faculty on the column
not used to designate the time frame. Information cards are then
labeled for use in constructing the mosaic, with a separate
card being designed for each individual course and section. For

---

[4]Bossing and Cramer, pp. 136-39. Reprinted by permission of the publisher.

example, three sections of English 2 would require three separate cards.

| English 2A | English 2B | English 2C |

The Conflict Sheet. A large amount of the "trial-and-error" involved in the mosaic method can be eliminated through a device known as the *conflict sheet,* which might be better called a conflict resolution sheet. In the conventional scheduling process, this device is simply a special sheet of paper lined in such a way that it will permit formation of a matrix that can then be used to locate individual student's course conflicts. This is illustrated in Figure 3.12. *Only single section* courses should be

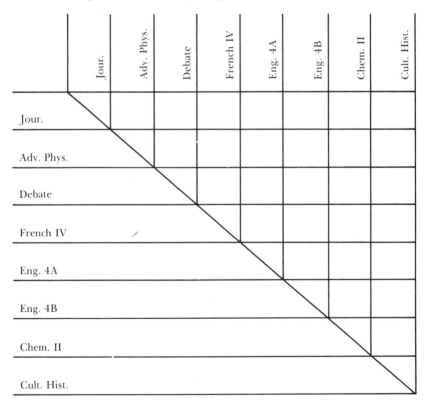

FIGURE 3.12. Portion of a Conflict Sheet.

plotted on the conflict sheet, since those courses having two or more similar sections can generally be arranged to avoid conflicts. Three basic steps for utilizing the conflict sheet follow:

1. Draw lines to form the matrix needed in a conflict. Beginning with the last grade in school (seniors, ninth graders, etc.), determine which single-section courses are offered at which grade level and list these along the left side of the matrix. Then match this listing with a second listing of the same courses at the top of the sheet. The conflict sheet can be as large as the total number of single sections offered. If the school operates with some form of ability grouping of students and only one ability-level section of each course is available, then each such special section should be considered a single-section course. A portion of a sample conflict sheet with course listings is shown in Figure 3.12.

2. After compilation of data obtained from the individual student registration schedule cards, the total tally of conflicts can be identified. These conflicts are precipitated when any two subjects are programmed during the same hour. A sample portion of senior registration cards may read as follows:

English 4A	Band
Journalism	French IV
Physical Education	
Cultural History	

A matrix is prepared as shown below. The first single-section course listed on the registration card is plotted against each other single-section course listed on the card. (English 4A would be plotted against each of the other single-section courses on the card.) If the lines cross anywhere on the matrix, a conflict mark should be tallied in that square. An analysis of the following chart reveals the following conflicts: English 4A conflicts with journalism, French IV with English 4A, and journalism with French

IV. Again, these are single-section courses a student desired but which are offered during the same time period.

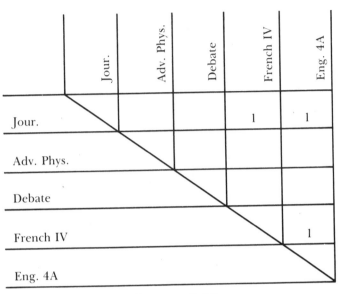

FIGURE 3.13

3. After each student registration card is checked for conflicts, and the total number of tallies is entered in each
square of the building-wide conflict sheet, a system of
priorities must then be developed. Those courses creating
the greatest number of schedule conflicts for students
may be programmed at different time periods in an effort
to minimize scheduling problems. Those courses still in
conflict then serve as the basic framework for the preparation of a mosaic schedule.

Students and secretaries can learn to tally conflict sheets very
quickly; even in large schools with enrollments of over 1500,
conflicts may be identified and tallied in approximately four or
five hours using the mosaic method.

Figure 3.14 reproduces a completed conflict sheet by Jacobson, Reavis, and Logsdon for a high school enrolling 225 Pupils

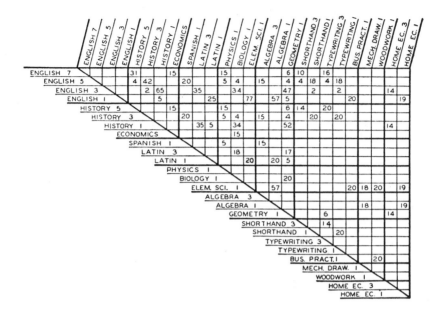

FIGURE 3.14. Conflict Sheet for a High School Enrolling 225 Pupils. All conflicts have been plotted. (Read: If English 7 and History 5 are placed at the same hour, 31 pupils will have a conflict; if English 7 and Economics are placed at the same hour, 15 will have a conflict; and so on.)[5]

as an example of how conflicts can be used to establish priorities for a Master Schedule.

As has been stated, those courses having the greatest number of conflicts are placed on the Master Schedule board first. The multiple-section courses are then added, and the various items can be juggled about further to iron out other difficulties that might be noticed. The next step is to be certain that all the information suggested earlier in the chapter is added to make the entire schedule completely comprehensive—a true master schedule.

---

[5]Jacobson, Reavis, and Logsdon, p. 73.

QUESTIONS AND SUGGESTIONS FOR STUDY

1. Using a checklist survey the schools near your area to determine how comprehensive their Master Schedules are. What
   factors predominate? What information is missing?

2. Design a conflict sheet. Take the single sections offered in
   your high school or junior high school and determine the
   number of conflicts you would have.

3. Explain the difference between a *teaching* schedule and a
   registration schedule.

4. Discuss the differences between an elementary and secondary master schedule.

SELECTED REFERENCES

Anderson, Lester W. "What Is the Most Effective Way of Arranging
    the Length and Use of the Class Period?" *The Bulletin of the
    NASSP* (April 1959): 162.
Jacobson, Paul B.; Reavis, William C.; and Logsdon, James D. *The
    Effective School Principal,* 2d ed. Englewood Cliffs, New Jersey:
    Prentice-Hall, 1963, Chapter 4, "Making a School Schedule."
Linder, Ivan H., and Gunn, Henry M. *Secondary Administration:
    Problems and Practices.* Columbus, Ohio: Charles E. Merrill Pub-
    lishing Co., 1963, Chapter 11, "Schedule Construction and Regis-
    tration."
Otto, Henry J., and Sanders, David C. *Elementary School Organiza-
    tion,* 4th ed. New York: Appleton-Century-Crofts, 1964, Chapters
    2 and 3, "Curriculum Issues" and "Organization for Instruction."
Ovard, Glen F. *Administration of the Changing Secondary School.*
    New York: Macmillan, 1966, Chapters 6 and 7, "The Annual Cycle
    —Beginning and Ending the School Year" and "Schedule-Making."

Chapter Four

Scheduling Instructional Activities in the Elementary School

The elementary school organized around self-contained classrooms requires a less complex form of scheduling than does the departmentalized elementary or secondary school. In a sense, it is a type of *group* scheduling where each grade level is composed of self-contained classes or "courses" assigned to a specific number of students. Within these classes the teacher actually operates a small school-within-a-school in which all or a majority of the subjects are taught by that same teacher. The time units for the subjects are established within the self-contained unit and generally it is not necessary to coordinate what is programmed in one classroom with what happens in other classrooms in the school building with the exception of time for recess, lunch and special programs or courses.

Team-teaching or certain nongrading patterns may be perceived as "schools-within-a school" combined to form even larger "self-contained" teaching units. As soon as a portion of the curriculum is organized departmentally, the scheduling process becomes more complex and important.

Effective organization of the teaching-learning process in the elementary school is very necessary and requires careful planning. Some major areas of instructional programming concerns of elementary schools operating self-contained classroom are

1. Registration
2. Teacher load
3. Teacher competencies (qualifications and interest)
4. Room, building, and facility characteristics
5. Organization of patterns for curricular offerings (e.g., nongraded classes), including instructional strategies
6. Time allotments, including start and end of school day and units of time for each learning experience
7. Scheduling of special events (plays, recess, safety patrol, etc.)
8. Preparation of room schedules
9. Preparation of a master schedule

REGISTRATION

Registration and enrollment procedures were reviewed in Chapter Two and illustrative forms presented. This process is vital to the school and the placement of learners in appropriate grade level or classes. Parental involvement during the registration process is necessary because of the age of the children and their inability to provide the needed information.

Although many elementary schools have a preregistration in the spring, they may utilize differing procedures to obtain various types of information. In some instances, students and parents are asked to preregister on a separate form each spring. If the student has been attending regularly, his previous records are checked, and the scheduled conference tends to become a placement of the youngster for the coming year. The completion of promotion lists and the forwarding of them to the principal and next year's teacher are actually forms of preregistration by groups. Quite often, the teachers of the grade levels involved meet to discuss individual students and, sometimes, to exchange particular youngsters. A sample promotion list, or preregistration sheet, follows in Figure 4.1.

In areas where there are a large number of migrant children in the school population, these lists may need to be rechecked every four to six weeks for deletions and additions. In all cases, maintenance of an up-to-date cumulative record form is of vital importance.

Clark County School District

Promotion List, Elementary K-6

Assigning School_____ Receiving School_____Date_____

Class Section No._____ Total Number_____Teacher Assigned_____

Assigning Teacher	Name of pupil	Age Next September 1st		Assignment	Last Basic or Supplementary Method Reader Completed
		Yr.	Mo.	Grade and Level	
	1.				
	2.				
	3.				
	4.				
	5.				
	6.				
	7.				
	8.				
	9.				

FIGURE 4.1. Promotion List. (Reproduced by courtesy of Clark County School District, Las Vegas, Nevada.)

TEACHER LOAD

In the self-contained classroom, computation of teacher load by the use of any specific formula is difficult. The teacher is assigned a group of from twenty-five to forty youngsters and often has the total responsibility for them the entire day. When discussing pupil-teacher ratio, it should be made quite clear to district patrons what the term implies. Parents should realize that a thirty-to-one pupil-teacher ratio in the elementary school may mean either an average of thirty pupils per teacher or that all the administrators, counselors and special supervisors are added to this figure. The class load should be based upon the actual number of students for which each teacher is responsible. Although a specific guide, such as the Douglass formula, has not been worked out for elementary teachers, a checklist and point chart could be developed from the following factors to provide some comparative data on individual teachers work load.

Factors to Consider in the Elementary Teacher Work Load

1. Number of students in class (specified by several state laws)
2. Number of separate subjects taught by the teacher
3. Average number of pupils *times* the number of subjects taught each week (e.g., 30 students X five different subjects = 150 students daily)
4. The pupil activities sponsored
5. Special administrative duties, such as playground, hall monitor, student register, etc.
6. Participation in professional activities (including P.T.A. which often requires considerable extra time at the elementary school level)
7. Participation in political and community affairs
8. Participation in special projects and programs
9. Sociological atmosphere of the community or attendance area (e.g., students from culturally deprived areas require more individual time.)

Calculations of these measures generally result in a work week of a specified number of hours. Findings of studies conducted regarding this matter have estimated a work week ranging from forty-six to fifty-three hours.

One of the problems elementary teachers have had is that almost no time is available during the school day for preparation for teaching. Too often, these teachers must be with learners in their classrooms from morning through afternoon, including recesses and lunch hours. Consequently, little or no time is found during school hours either for attending to necessary personal matters or for classroom preparation. This key concern, expressed by many elementary teachers, should be considered by principals during instructional programming. Teaming of teacher talents, partial departmentalization, and the use of teaching specialists in physical education, music, and art has alleviated this problem to a degree.

Assigning the Teacher

By mid-year (January or February), information on teacher preferences for teaching assignments by grade level, subject matter, or teaching area preferences for the following year should be gathered and summarized. If time permits, each teacher should be consulted personally about these preferences. Teachers do experience changes in attitudes, and preferences may shift during the year; nonetheless, a teacher's interests in a particular grade level or subject area should be given serious consideration, assuming, of course, that the teacher is qualified in the area of preference and that other specified school needs receive priority over such a request. Any denials should be explained and discussed.

Again, certain common sense factors in teacher assignment should be considered. Among these are age, physical ability, interest, demonstrated capabilities, health, availability and special skills.

Organization of the Curriculum and Schedule Patterns

As stated earlier, the curriculum design determines and controls program arrangement. The three basic elementary curricular plans described by Otto and Sanders were described in Chapter Three. These plans included subjects taught in isolation, broad fields, and activity or experience. Otto and Sanders' projection

Subjects-Taught-in-Isolation

8:45- 9:00	Management duties / Opening exercises
9:00- 9:35	Arithmetic
9:35-10:00	Reading & literature
10:00-10:15	Spelling
10:15-10:30	Recess
10:30-11:00	Geography (assembly programs once a week)
11:00-11:30	History (current events and civics once a week)
11:30-11:45	Music
11:45-12:00	Handwriting
12:00- 1:00	Lunch / Free Play
1:00- 1:30	Science
1:30- 2:00	Grammar and composition
2:00- 2:15	Recess
2:15- 3:00	Health (twice a week) / Special interests, homemaking, industrial arts (three times a week)

Broad Fields

8:45- 9:00	Management duties / Health inspection / Planning
9:00-10:30	Social and civic education activities (including all related phases of language arts, music, art, and other associated activities)
10:30-11:00	Physical education
11:00-12:00	Arithmetic (including related language arts)
12:00- 1:00	Lunch and rest period
1:00- 2:00	Science and Health (including related language arts, music, art and other associated activities)
2:00- 2:25	Music (Tuesday and Thursday)
2:00- 3:00	Art (Monday and Wednesday)
2:25- 3:00	Individual help and independent work (Tuesday and Thursday)
2:00- 3:00	Special interest clubs (Friday)

Activity or Experience

Time	Activity
8:45- 9:15	Management duties / Health inspection / Show and tell / Planning
9:15-10:30	Time used as planned
10:30-11:00	Physical education
11:00-12:00	Time used as planned
12:00- 1:00	Lunch and rest period
1:00- 2:40	Time used as planned
2:40- 3:00	Evaluation and clean-up / Plans for tomorrow

FIGURE 4.2. Sample Daily Programs with Three Different Types of Curriculum Design.[1]

for daily schedules for these three curriculum designs are given in Figure 4.2. Otto and Sanders have cautioned that these hypothetical schedules usually need some modification before they can be applied to local situations.

The organization for *nongrading* varies considerably from this conventional pattern. In many instances, schools will eliminate rigid designations for only two or three grades during which classification of pupils may be based on the pupil's reading level as is done in Figure 4.2. As a consequence, some schools organize their programs using achievement levels or phases in a particular subject to group students across several grade levels, while others group the levels or phases *within* the self-contained classroom unit. If a multiple-graded plan is used, it requires still another organizational pattern. The overall operation of nongraded programs has been described in detail by Goodlad and Anderson in a book entitled *The Nongraded Elementary School.*[2]

Instructional organizations emphasizing individually guided education, such as found in the multi-unit elementary schools or in the ipi (individually prescribed instruction) schools, follow an even looser and more flexible school schedule. The time for the start of the school day, its termination, and special breaks are scheduled, but the study flow from one subject to another may not be. The exceptions to this rule would be periods reserved for physical education, art, and similar learning experiences.

The placement of students is generally done in the spring, with teachers receiving test information about each child on individual cards. Some schools have moved toward using marginal key sort cards to assist teachers in locating specific information about one child or a group of children at a moment's notice. A sample profile placement card is illustrated in Figure 4.3.

[1]Henry J. Otto and David C. Sanders. *Elementary School Organization and Administration,* 4th ed. (New York: Appleton-Century-Crofts, 1964), p. 66. Copyright © 1964 by Meredith Publishing Co. Reprinted by permission of Appleton-Century-Crofts, Educational Division, Meredith Corporation.

[2]John I. Goodlad and Robert H. Anderson, *The Nongraded Elementary School* (Burlingame: Harcourt, Brace, and World, Inc., 1963), pp. 61-79.

1964 - 1965
Old Bethpage School

Child's name _____

Yrs. _____ Mo. _____
Age

IRI Level _____

Check where appropriate and comment (back).

Emotional _____

Health _____

Speech _____

Social

Mature _____ Immature _____

Isolate _____

Leader _____

Learning Rate

Slow _____

Average _____

Above Aver. _____

Sending Teacher _____

Receiving Teacher _____

FIGURE 4.3. Profile Card: Nongraded Program[3]

Team Teaching plans also vary considerably, and the consequent arrangement of a schedule changes with the type of project being used. If the teams remain within the one grade level, the problem is less complex than in a situation in which the teams are assigned by subject areas across two or more grade levels. Teachers become involved more directly in the administrative aspects of these programs and tend to work out the details of time and placement on a daily or weekly basis so as to provide a great deal of individual flexibility. As a consequence, specific room schedules are not always available, a factor that often can be confusing to visitors who are accustomed

---

[3]Lillian Glogau and Murray Fessel, *The Nongraded Primary School* (West Nyack, N.Y.: Parker Publishing Company, Inc., 1967), p. 26. Copyright © 1967 by Parker Publishing Co., Inc. Reprinted by permission of the publisher.

to the traditional time schedule of the self-contained classroom. (Figure 4.4 illustrates a daily nongraded reading schedule in the Clark County School System.)

Daily Plan				
8:25 - 9:10 *In the library*				
	M	*T*	*W*	*T*	*F*
Group I	Independent Reading	Listening Center**	Text* and Conference	Overhead Projector**	S.R.A. and Macmillan Spectrum
Group II	S.R.A. and Macmillan Spectrum	Independent Reading	Listening Center	Text and Conference	Overhead Projector
Group III	Overhead Projector	S.R.A. and Macmillan Spectrum	Independent Reading	Listening Center	Text and Conference
Group IV	Text and Conference	Overhead Projector	S.R.A. and Macmillan Spectrum	Independent Reading	Listening Center
Group V	Listening Center	Text and Conference	Overhead Projector	S.R.A. and Macmillan Spectrum	Independent Reading

9:10 - 9:30   *In the classroom:*

McCall Crabbs Speed Reading exercises	Book sharing
Projects	Puzzles
Games that teach reading	Phonics drill

*Each student progresses at his own rate of speed and checks his own work. A test is given after each unit to determine which skills need to be retaught.

**Listening Center – (teacher made tapes)
Listening skills
Comprehension
Direct recall
Structural analysis
Phonetic analysis
Dictionary skills

Overhead Projector – Drills and skills
Comprehension
Dictionary skills
Structural analysis
Phonetic analysis

FIGURE 4.4. Schedule for Individualized Reading Program. (Reproduced by courtesy of C. P. Squires Elementary School, Clark County School District, Las Vegas, Nevada.)

Figure 4.5 illustrates a summary schedule of Reading Instructional Level for 207 first year primary children in the Old Bethpage School in Plainview, Long Island.

June 1965

First Year Primary

(207 children)

Level 3	One child
Level 4	Thirty-six children
Level 5	Fifty children
Level 6	Sixty-four children
Level 7	Forty-three children
Level 8	Four children
Level 9	Six children
Level 10	—
Level 11	One child
Level 12	Two children

FIGURE 4.5. Reading Instruction Level for Primary Children: Nongraded Program of Old Bethpage School in Plainview, Long Island.[4]

This program involves both nongrading and team-teaching across traditional grade levels. Scheduling consequently is structured on the basis of test scores and the use of varying group sizes within a team range.

Glogau and Fessel have also illustrated a grouping chart for nongrading that is designed for pupil placement and based on reading level. This chart is reproduced in Figure 4.6.

TIME ALLOTMENTS

The bases for time allotments generally include the State Department of Education minimum requirements, district policy and, at times, the local attendance unit policy. The time units and modules are often determined cooperatively with the teacher of each room, team or phase and then recorded in some form.

The principal should have a summary or master chart of all time requirements and assignments and may wish to forward a

---

[4]Lillian Glogau and Murray Fessel, pp. 86-87.

CLASSES																		
Reading Level	A	B	C	D	E	F	G	H	I	J	K	L	M	N	O	P	Q	
Two	5	5	5	5	5	5	5+ (1)											
Three	9	7	7	8	8	5+ (1)	6	(2+) [1]										
Four	11	12	12	12	12	(11)	(12)	(8+) [3]	(12+) [1]	[11]	(1)		[1]					
Five								(13)	(7)	(8)	(12)	[9]			(2)			
Six								(7)	(8)	(7)	[10]							
Seven										(6)	(9)	(7+) [3]	[11]	[6]				
Eight												(4+) [3]	[9]	[9]				
Nine												(5)	(9)	[12]	[10]	[11]		
Ten														[10]				
Eleven																(2+) [7]		
Twelve															[8]	(1+) [8]		

Code
Not Circled – Six Year Olds
Circled – Seven Year Olds
Squared – Eight Year Olds

FIGURE 4.6. Nongraded Grouping Chart of Old Bethpage School, Plainview, Long Island.[5]

chart of minimum state and district time perimeters to individual faculty members for planning purposes. This summary or planning time chart might be managed in several ways. Figure 4.7 illustrates subject structure schedule that is comprehensive and covers an entire school.

[5]Glogau and Fessel, p. 25.

Daily Time	K	1	2	3	4	5	6
Total Minute Daily							
Total Recess Daily							
Total Lunch Daily							
Minute- Reading							
Minute- Science							
Minute- Social Studies							

FIGURE 4.7. Summary Time Schedule Sheet

This summary time schedule sheet is a helpful device in preparing final district and State Department reports. Charts can be designed by grade level, by teacher, or by subject area, depending upon the data desired. It also provides helpful information in calculating teacher load.

SCHEDULING OF SPECIAL EVENTS

The dates and time of special plays and related extra class activities are generally listed on the weekly, monthly, or Master Calendar. On the other hand, recesses, assemblies, safety patrol and other activities specifically scheduled within the daily program must be considered a part of the daily schedule. In some instances, an all-school assembly schedule period is worked out, and each teacher has a revised schedule to follow on assembly days. The same situation is true for minimum day schedules where five to ten minutes are subtracted from each session so that students can be released earlier. In some schools, the teachers are given the time range for special schedules, and they, in turn, adjust their daily room schedule to that time range.

The scheduling of school safety patrols can create various problems for a small number of students. One principal in a California school made an informal survey of the time his patrol boys were out of class and checked their achievement during the time they were on duty. Since his school utilized a "slip-schedule" with two different starting times, two different lunch times, and two different ending times, he found that during the four to six weeks these boys were on duty, they lost considerable time from class. As an apparent consequence, their achievement dropped noticeably while on duty. These are factors which principals should consider in scheduling special projects and activities.

Scheduling Lunch Hours

Generally, scheduling lunch hours for self-contained classrooms does not present a major problem. Though the lunchroom may be small and two or more "waves" of students may be required, the children can be assigned a lunch time by groups of rooms. Thus, in a three-"wave" plan, three groups of children can be scheduled in a twenty or thirty minute sequence for lunch in a small cafeteria or lunchroom. Even in semi-departmentalized or platoon systems, children can be scheduled by advisors or homerooms. In smaller rural schools, the pupils often still eat in the regular classroom.

Many elementary schools schedule a ten or fifteen minute milk or snack break in both the morning and afternoon sessions. The system varies. Some schools release all the children at the same time so that they either report to a central area or remain in the classroom; others release the students by "waves" similar to the lunch hour scheduling. If the school is totally departmentalized (e.g., a middle school), then the lunch schedule should be structured as in the secondary level school.

ROOM ASSIGNMENT CHARTS

A room assignment chart somewhat similar to that suggested for secondary principals later in this chapter should be designed and utilized in making specific room assignments. In flexible programs, a room and facility chart would be most helpful for planning.

Room capacity, available facilities, and special features of each room should be described on a master record in the principal's office. Building utilization studies provide data helpful in determining how to revise room assignment, when to request additional space, and what special space needs may be necessary for the implementation of curricular programs. Leavitt has used the following formula in studying utilization of school facilities, space, and personnel:[6]

$$\frac{\text{(Actual)}}{\text{(Theoretical)}} \quad \frac{\text{Number of Classes} \ \times \ \text{Number of Periods} \ \times \ \text{Minutes Per Period}}{\text{Number of Classes} \ \times \ \text{Number of Periods} \ \times \ \text{Minutes Per Period}} = \begin{array}{l} \text{Percent of} \\ \text{Educational} \\ \text{Efficiency} \end{array}$$

Normally, elementary interchangeable stations operate at a 100 percent efficiency utilization ratio, while special station efficiency ratios should be 85 percent or better. Figure 4.8 illustrates Leavitt's compilation of space utilization.

Principals should exercise care in assigning rooms to classes by checking furniture size, capacity, location with respect to noise, and accessability for students, faculty and special equipment.

ROOM SCHEDULES

Individual room schedules are usually constructed in the fall after final registration has occurred. Quite often, the first few weeks become a trial plan for this schedule, and several revisions may be necessary before a relatively permanent schedule can be constructed. However, teachers should feel that they have authority to operate within a flexible framework at all times.

---

[6]Urban J. D. Leavitt, "Elementary School Size Relationships" (Doctoral Dissertation, University of Texas, 1960).

[7]Ibid.

Plan	Total Class Minutes	Opening Exercises	Closing Exercises	Prelunch Period	Postlunch Period	Lunch	Total Available Time	Number of 25-minute Periods	Percent of Utilization	Number of 30-minute Periods	Percent of Utilization
A	390	–	–	–	–	–	390	15	96.2	13	100.0
B	390	15	–	–	–	–	375	15	96.2	12	92.3
C	390	15	15	–	–	–	360	14	89.7	12	92.3
D	390	15	15	30	–	–	330	13	83.3	11	84.6
E	390	15	15	30	30	–	300	12	77.0	10	77.0
F	390	15	15	30	30	30	270	10	64.1	9	69.2

FIGURE 4.8. Utilization of the Separate Gymnasium[7]

Principals should inform teachers of state time requirements and district policy, and, if the program involves team-teaching or nongrading, cooperative decisions are then made. Each teacher should confer with the principal regarding his room schedule, and a copy of the schedule should be retained by the principal. A room schedule is then posted both in each classroom and in the school office as a guide for pupils and teachers.

An exception exists in the kindergarten schedule. Kindergarten schedules are usually quite flexible. Although teachers utilize a general daily outline, they must remain adaptable to any situation. Figure 4.9 presents a typical kindergarten room schedule.

Finally, Figure 4.10 illustrates a conventional self-contained classroom schedule, while Figure 4.11 depicts a partially departmentalized or platooned room schedule. The art section of the platooned schedule is illustrated in Figure 4.12.

Room schedules and special teacher schedules become considerably more complex when a nongrading program is used. Special preparation times, team or group meetings, and planning sessions must all be accounted for in the schedule. This type of schedule must be constructed cooperatively in order to permit incorporation of the many facets of such a program. Figure 4.13 illustrates a Special Teacher Schedule in the Old Bethpage School, which employs a nongrading plan.

THE MASTER SCHEDULE

At the elementary school level, the Master Schedule is primarily a summation of the various room and special schedules. Illustration of how these schedules for self-contained classrooms might be combined were presented in Chapter Three.

Nongrading and team programs are more difficult to summarize, but large charts picturing the progress of groups of children could be constructed and utilized as an information resource. This could be done either by rooms or by subunits (primary, intermediate) in the total school program. Figure 4.14 illustrates a principal's chart for the primary levels in the nongraded Parkway School in Plainfield, New York.

Clark County School District

Daily Program

School C. P. Squires Elementary

Date _____

8:30 – 10:45 class

Room ___1___ Grade ___Kindergarten___

Time	Monday	Tuesday	Wednesday	Thursday	Friday
8:30 – 8:45	Opening Exercises:	Pledge of allegiance, roll call, health inspection, conversation and planning for the day.			
8:45 – 9:05	Music and Rhythms:	Songs – singing, listening and creating.			
9:05 – 9:30	Physical Education:	Supervised outdoor activities and use of equipment.			
9:30 – 10:20	Social Program and Activities:	Day by day interests from experiences in living together in the home, school and neighborhood (individual or group). 1. Plans – stimulating curiosity and interests. 2. Participation – making, doing, experimenting, creating, solving problems and improving techniques. 3. Evaluation – of achievements and adjustments. Further plans. 4. Care of materials. Clean up time.			
10:20 – 10:40	Language Arts:	Appreciation and enjoyment. Stories, poems, finger plays, rhymes, dramatic play, pictures, things of interest and beauty.			
10:40 – 10:45	Preparation for Dismissal:	Talk about our day and safety rules. Pin on notes for parents.			
10:45	Dismissal.				

FIGURE 4.9. Kindergarten Daily Room Schedule. (Reproduced by courtesy of C. P. Squires Elementary School, Clark County School District, Las Vegas, Nevada.)

Clark County School District

Teacher _____ School _____ C. P. Squires

Room ___13___ Grade ___5___ Date _____

Daily Program

Time	Monday	Tuesday	Wednesday	Thursday	Friday
8:20	News — Pledge	Stories — Pledge	Reports — Pledge	Poems — Pledge	Book Report
8:30	Phonics	Phonics	Phonics	Phonics	Phonics
8:40	Reading	Reading	Reading	Reading	Reading
9:30	Arithmetic	Arithmetic	Arithmetic	Arithmetic	Arithmetic
10:15	Break	Break	Break	Break	Break
10:25	Science	Science	Science	Science	Science
10:50	English	English	Library	English	English

Spelling-Writing

11:20	Spelling	Spelling	Library	Spelling	Spelling
11:40	Writing	Writing	Library	Writing	Writing
11:55	Lunch	Lunch	Lunch	Lunch	Lunch
12:40	Soc. Studies	Soc. Studies	Soc. Studies	Soc. Studies	Soc. Studies
			Class Meeting		
1:25	P. E.	P. E.	P. E.	P. E.	P. E.
2:00	Music	Music	Art	Music	Art
2:35	Dismissal	Dismissal	Dismissal	Dismissal	Dismissal

FIGURE 4.10. Conventional Self-Contained Room Schedule. (Reproduced by Courtesy of C. P. Squires Elementary School, Clark County School District, Las Vegas, Nevada.)

Room 27 — Teachers Schedule

8:45 - 9:00	Assemble with home room on blacktop for flag ceremony
8:50 - 9:00	Pupil-teacher planning
9:00 - 9:30	Science, Soc. St., Health and Safety Monday 9:00 - 9:25 Library Room 35
9:30 - 9:50	Writing Conference and/or Preparation*
9:50 - 10:25	Arithmetic
10:25 - 10:30	Break Tuesday 9:00 - 9:35 Art Room 8
10:30 - 12:00	Reading, Physical Education, and Music Conference and/or Preparation

	Monday - Tuesday - Wednesday - Friday			*Thursday*		
Group	A	B	C	A	B	C
10:30 - 11:00	R	PE	M	R	PE	L
11:00 - 11:30	PE	M	R	PE	L	R
11:30 - 12:00	M	R	PE	L	R	PE

12:00 - 12:35	Lunch 12:35 Meet home room on blacktop and proceed to classroom
12:40 - 12:50	Story Time
12:50 - 1:30	English
1:30 - 1:35	Break
1:35 - 2:30	Reading, Phonics, and Creative Writing
2:30 - 2:50	Spelling
2:50 - 3:00	Cleanup and Evaluation
3:00	Dismissal

FIGURE 4.11. Semi-Departmentalized (Platoon) Room Schedule. (Reproduced by courtesy of Laura Dearing Elementary School, Clark County School District, Las Vegas, Nevada.)

Art	Monday	Tuesday	Wednesday	Thursday	Friday
9:00 to 9:55	Room 26 (3)	Room 27 (5)	Room 28 (3)	Room 29 (3)	Room 4 (2)
10:00 to 10:55	Room 22 (2)	Room 23 (2)	Room 24 (2)	Room 25 (2)	Room 5 (1)
11:00 to 11:55	Room 17 (1)	Room 18 (1)	Room 19 (1)	Room 20 (1)	Room 21 (1)
12:40* to 1:40	4-3	6-3	5-3	5-2	6-1
1.40 to 2:10	Break				
2:10 to 3:10	6-2	4-4	5-1	4-1	4-2

*Classes grouped by ability. The first number is the grade level; the second, ability level.

FIGURE 4.12. Art Schedule for Semi-Departmentalized Program. (Reproduced by courtesy of Laura Dearing Elementary School, Clark County School District, Las Vegas, Nevada.)

A sample organizational and operational general Master Schedule for team-teaching at the intermediate level which has been employed by the Pittsburgh Schools, is illustrated in Figure 4.15. Children were scheduled into homerooms on the basis of reading ability and were team-taught in academic subject areas. Primary youngsters spent approximately 75 percent of their time in self-contained classroom situations.

Numerous samples of different schedules are available, but many of these are applicable to only one specific situation. The samples illustrated in this chapter were presented for the purpose of guiding rather than restricting schedule construction and should be examined with this in mind.

OLD BETHPAGE SCHOOL SPECIAL TEACHER SCHEDULE

FIGURE 4.13. Special Teacher Schedule: Nongraded of Old Bethpage School, Plainview, Long Island, New York. [8]

Class	1	2	3	4	5	6	7	8	9	10	11	12	Totals
A	8	13											21
B	8	13											21
*C	8	12											20
D			12	12									24
E			16	8									24
*F			9	7	8								24
*G				8	9	9							26
*H					16	9							25
*I					13	12							25
J					7	8	12						27
K					9	9	10						28
L						8	13	6					27
M									9	9	9		27
N									9	9	9		27
O										5	12	10	27
P										6	12	10	28
Totals	24	38	37	35	54	63	35	6	18	29	42	20	401

*Indicates inter-age mixing.

FIGURE 4.14. Schedule for Nongraded Primary School of The Parkway School, Plainfield, New York[9]

[8]Glogau and Fessel, p. 172.

[9]Frank R. Dufay, *Ungrading the Elementary School* (West Nyack, N.Y. Parker Publishing Company, Inc., 1966), p. 50. Reprinted by permission of the publisher.

The elementary schedule and the work load of the elementary teacher needs additional study. It has been a relatively simple operation in the past, but with larger enrollments and the innovation and adaptation of new programs, this situation is no longer true. The door has been opened for research in the technical operation of the elementary school schedule.

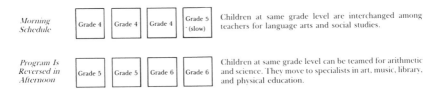

Morning Schedule | Grade 4 | Grade 4 | Grade 4 | Grade 5 (slow) | Children at same grade level are interchanged among teachers for language arts and social studies.

Program Is Reversed in Afternoon | Grade 5 | Grade 5 | Grade 6 | Grade 6 | Children at same grade level can be teamed for arithmetic and science. They move to specialists in art, music, library, and physical education.

FIGURE 4.15. General Outline, Team Teaching Plan of the Pittsburgh School System[10]

QUESTIONS AND SUGGESTIONS FOR STUDY

1. Why is the conventional elementary school program simpler to schedule than a departmentalized secondary school program?

2. Describe factors which cause elementary schedule construction to become more complex.

3. How can the computer be utilized in elementary school scheduling?

4. Describe the three different programs identified by Henry Otto and David Sanders.

5. How are students selected and assigned to phases or levels in a nongraded program?

6. What is meant by a semi-departmentalized or platoon program?

---

[10]Maurie Hillson, *Change and Innovation in Elementary School Organization* (New York: Holt, Rinehart, and Winston, 1965), p. 197. Originally published in *Annual Report of the Superintendent of Schools* by the Board of Education, Pittsburgh, Pa. Reprinted by the Board of Public Education, Pittsburgh, Pa.

7. Visit an elementary school using the conventional self-contained classroom plan. Collect the various room and special schedules and construct a Master Schedule. Outline the procedures for determining the room schedule in this school.

8. Visit an elementary school employing a nongrading and/or team-teaching plan. Design a master schedule for this school. How do the procedures differ from the self-contained school?

9. Make a room efficiency utilization study for an elementary school using the formula reported in this chapter.

SELECTED REFERENCES

Dufay, Frank R. *Ungrading the Elementary School.* West Nyack, New York: Parker Publishing Co., 1966. Chapters 2, 3, 4, and 5 deal with organizing and scheduling the nongraded school.

Glogau, Lillian, and Fessel, Murray. *The Nongraded Primary School.* West Nyack, New York: Parker Publishing Co., 1967. A specific report on one school utilizing nongrading as a basis for implementation of curricular organization.

Goodlad, John I., and Anderson, Robert H. *The Nongraded Elementary School,* rev. ed. New York: Harcourt, Brace, and World, Inc., 1963. A comprehensive book on the nongraded elementary school concept.

Hillson, Maurie. "Departmentalized and Semidepartmentalized Grouping Plans," "Team-Teaching, Team-Learning, Coordinate and Collaborative Teaching," and "Nongrading." In *Change and Innovation in Elementary School Organization,* Parts III, IV, and V. New York: Holt, Rinehart, and Winston, 1965.

Otto, Henry J., and Sanders, David C. "Organization for Instruction," and "Provisions for Administering the Educational Program." In *Elementary School Organization and Administration,* 4th ed., Chapters 3 and 11. New York: Appleton-Century-Crofts, 1964.

Chapter Five

Scheduling Instructional Activities in the Secondary Schools

Instructional programming in the secondary school demands numerous policy resolutions, curricular decisions, and rather precise sequencing. The end product is an organizational chart of instructional activities to describe the practical interaction of philosophy, people, and school experiences. The process of obtaining this product has a scientific base, but it also has an important artistic component.

DETERMINING POLICY

Before the actual beginning of instructional programming, certain key policy decisions must be reviewed or formulated. A faculty committee, such as an instructional programming advisory council, may assist in determining basic principles which reflect the philosophy of the school and its staff. Linder and Gunn outline the areas which should be clarified before building the schedule.

1. The time of the opening and closing of school should be established, together with the number and length of class periods. Time should be provided for passing between classes and for warning bells at the opening of school in the

    morning and the resumption of classes after the lunch hour. One or more lunch periods should be established.

2. The pattern of course offerings, including both required and elective courses, should be established. If such controls on pupil-choice as majors and minors are in effect, these should be clearly indicated.

3. A plan should be set up for assigning pupils to class sections. Are pupils to be given any choice of class period or teacher? If so, how is this controlled to prevent overloading of certain periods or to provide some balance of class size between teachers of the same subject who vary in their popularity with pupils?

4. To what extent is pupil choice of subjects related to such variations in graduation requirements as those for the general, the vocational, or the college-preparatory diploma?

5. Is ability grouping followed in any of the required courses? If so, by what means is the placement of pupils in these groups determined and who is responsible for such assignments?

6. What is a standard teaching load in the different subject fields, including the number of separate preparations?

7. What maximum and minimum class sizes are established for the different subject fields? How is such control exercised and who decides when an over-load class section is to be divided into two sections?

8. What consideration is given the subject preparation, experience, and preference of the teacher?

9. What type of advisory service in program choice is provided pupils? Is it the policy of the school to require parental approval on pupil's program choice and program changes?[1]

Other criteria vital to the smooth assembly of a schedule will be considered in this chapter. These will not include the process of *registration* which was outlined in Chapter Two, and various *types* of school schedules, which were described in Chapter Three. Many criteria are common to both elementary and secondary school programs; however, the very nature of a departmentalized program immediately increases the complexity of

---

[1]Ivan H. Linder and Henry M. Gunn, *Secondary School Administration: Problems and Practices* (Columbus, Ohio: Charles E. Merrill Publishing Co., 1963), pp. 166-167. Reprinted by permission of the publisher.

scheduling and, consequently, requires consideration of criteria unique to this type of organizational plan.

TEACHER TIME AND TEACHER LOAD

The National Education Association conducted a study to determine how the secondary teacher spent his time. They found that the typical secondary teacher was in the classroom for twenty-six periods per week, with class duration of fifty-five minutes. This teacher found an average of twenty-seven pupils in each class, and his average total pupil responsibility per day was 156 students. More than one-half of the teachers surveyed allocated one period per day for preparation.

Teacher Time. Ninety-three percent of the teachers devoted more than one-half of their teaching time to a single subject; two percent taught two subjects, while the remainder taught more than two subjects. In addition, teachers devoted an average of 13.3 hours per week to correcting papers and performing related routine tasks. Still other duties required an average of nine hours per week.[2]

A comparison of the 1950 and 1960 NEA studies indicates that during that decade a slight drop occurred in the number of extra assignments given to teachers. Studies conducted several years ago indicate that teachers preferred the challenge of preparing for two different types of instructional challenge to having either just one preparation or more than two. As a rule, three and even four preparations were preferred to a situation where the same subject and grade level was taught five periods per day. Several informal surveys of a number of teachers conducted by the author during the past five years tend to support this data.

Teacher Load. The mislabeling and misuse of this term seems to affect teacher morale more than any other factor directly related to scheduling. As was stated earlier, the term *teacher load* too often is considered to be synonymous with *pupil-teacher ratio.* For example, some educators feel that a teacher

---

[2] *The American School Teacher* (Washington: National Education Association, Research Monograph M2, April 1963).

with five classes with twenty-two pupils in each class has a lighter load than a teacher who has five sections with thirty students per class no matter how many other responsibilities the first teacher might have. Obviously, other factors should be considered before any generalizations are made. To illustrate, it should be made clear to both teachers and the public whether a ratio of twenty-nine-to-one does or does not include all personnel in a given school in its computation. It should be remembered that these figures depend upon school policy and, too often, upon the financial ability of the district.

If an eight-hour day is considered normal for the teacher, it would be interesting to compute just what this might mean for the teacher-load factor.

1. The eight-hour day equals 480 minutes.
2. Assume that there are five periods of fifty-five minutes each. (Actually, there are approxmiately sixty minutes per period when time is allowed between periods.) The total time for teaching, then, would be 300 minutes, with 180 minutes left.
3. One hundred minutes would be allowed for lunch, preparation period, conference, extra class duties and personal matters; eighty minutes would be left.
4. Eighty minutes would be left for actual classroom preparation; when eighty is divided by five preparations, there would be approximately sixteen minutes left for preparation for each class.

These figures do not include time for the grading of additional papers and assignments. Assume, for example, that a teacher has 150 students and assigns a test or a special paper. If he were to spend only ten minutes on each paper, it would mean a total of 1,500 minutes or twenty-five hours of work to be done on this assignment alone.

Bent and McCann have recommended that certain major elements be considered in determining teacher load. The following list has been adapted from these recommendations.

1. Total number of class sections per week
2. Average number of pupils per class

3. Subject taught
4. Number of preparations per day
5. Pupil activities sponsored
6. Amount of teacher participation in the administration of the school
7. Participation in professional activities
8. Sociological climate of the particular attendance unit
9. Participation in community or political activities[3]

Douglass has described similar factors and has added:

1. The nature of the subject taught and the consequent amount of time required for preparation; for marking papers and notebooks; and for arranging equipment, apparatus, and materials.
2. The personality of the pupils taught: tractability and range of individual difference in ability (factors very difficult to measure).
3. The age and maturity of the pupils taught and the consequent character of the subject matter.[4]

Regardless of the technique utilized, the principal is responsible for developing some type of job analysis of each position. He should attempt to determine what an effective work load is and then equalize this factor among his staff. One technique would be to develop a checklist and to assign an arbitrary point system containing the major elements of a teacher's work load listed on the previous page. Such a system would provide some common factor for load determination. Though not statistical in nature, it would provide an outline of the work loads of individual teachers so that adjustments could then be made in assignments.

The Douglass Formula. Another means of computing a teacher's work load is the formula developed by Harl Douglass and subsequently revised in part by Christian A. Jung, one of his doctoral advisees. The Douglass formula is based on the

---

[3]Rudyard K. Bent and Lloyd E. McCann, *Administration of Secondary Schools* (New York: McGraw-Hill Book Co., 1966), pp. 217-219. Reprinted by permission of the publisher and of Lloyd E. McCann.

[4]Harl Douglass, *Modern Administration of Secondary Schools* (Boston: Ginn and Company, Second edition, 1963), p. 79. Reprinted by permission of the author.

premise that the teaching load can be described in units which can then be compared. The unit of teaching load in the formula is theoretically equivalent to teaching a class of twenty-five pupils for one fifty-minute period, with time allowance for specific preparation. The weightings represent ratios based upon the average amount of time spent by large numbers of teachers of particular subjects when compared to the time spent on all high school subjects on all levels.[5]

The Douglass formula and the subject grade coefficients are described below.

Douglass Formula for Determining Teacher Load

$$TL = SC \qquad CP = \frac{Dup}{10} + \frac{NP - 25\,CP}{100} \quad \frac{PL + 50}{100} + .6\,PC \quad \frac{PL + 50}{100}$$

CP = Number of class periods spent in classroom per week.

Dup = Number of class periods spent per week in classroom teaching for which the preparation is very similar to that for some other section. (This figure does not include the original section.)

NP = Number of pupils in classes per week.

PC = Number of class periods spent per week in supervision of study hall, student activities, teacher's meetings, committee work, assisting in administrative or supervisory work or other co-operatives.

PL = Gross length of class periods in minutes.

    *Number of class periods spent in PE, music, or subjects requiring very little or no written work and paper grading.

    $NP = \dfrac{NP}{2}$

    **In applying the formula to double period classes — science lab, home economics, typing, art, music, shop, agriculture — use the following procedures:

    1. Count each double period as two periods (CP).

    2. Count each double period as one unit of duplicate preparation over and above any other allowance made for duplicate preparation.

    3. Count the number of pupils for each half of double periods.

Two sample problems illustrating application of the Douglass formula to a practical school program follows.

---

[5]Christian A. Jung, "Revision of Douglass Teaching Load Formula" (Ed.D dissertation, University of Colorado, 1950).

Grade Level	7 and 8	9	10-11-12
English	1.2	1.3	1.3
Art	1.0	1.0	1.0
Home Economics	1.0	1.0	1.1
Music	.9	1.0	1.0
Mathematics*	1.0	1.0	1.0
Agriculture	–	–	1.3
Industrial Arts	.9	.9	1.0
Physical Education	.8	.9	.9
Health	1.0	1.1	1.2
Business Subjects	1.0	1.0	1.0
Social Studies	1.1	1.2	1.2
Foreign Language	1.0	1.0	1.0
Science	1.1	1.2	1.2

*Use CSG of 1.1 for sections employing new mathematics or applied mathematics in course of study.

Subject Grade Coefficients for Use in Teaching Load Formula

Examples of Computation of Teaching Load

Following are the computations for a teacher of mathematics and biology whose load is as follows in a school with 55-minute periods:

a. Two sections of biology of 24 and 28 tenth-graders respectively, meeting five periods a week.

b. Two sections of ninth-grade algebra of 26 and 29 pupils, meeting five periods a week.

c. One section of twelfth-grade chemistry of 21 pupils, meeting seven periods a week, including two double periods.

d. A chemistry club averaging 60 minutes a week; service on committees averaging 48 minutes a week; P.T.A. and other miscellaneous duties averaging 20 minutes a week — total 128 minutes.

$$TL = SGC \left[CP - \frac{Dup.}{10} + \frac{(NP - 25CP)}{100} \right] \left[\frac{PL + 50}{100} \right] + \left[.6PC \right] \left[\frac{PL + 50}{100} \right]$$

---

[6]Harl R. Douglass, pp. 79-80. This table is a revised list forwarded by Douglass to the author in August, 1968. This list substituted for the original chart in the book by permission of the author.

For the biology classes:

$$1.1 \left[10 - \frac{5}{10} + \frac{260 - 250}{100}\right] \left[\frac{55 + 50}{100}\right] =$$

$$1.1 \ (10 - .5 + .1) \ (1.05) = 11.09$$

For the algebra classes:

$$1.0 \left[10 - \frac{5}{10} + \frac{275 - 250}{100}\right] \left[\frac{55 + 50}{100}\right] =$$

$$1 \ (10 - .5 + .25) \ (1.05) = 10.24$$

For the chemistry class:

$$1.1 \left[7 - \frac{2}{10} + \frac{147 - 175}{100}\right] \left[\frac{55 + 50}{100}\right] =$$

$$1.1 \ (7 - .2 - .28) \ (1.05) = 7.53$$

For the co-operative or extra-teaching duties:

$$6 \left[\frac{60 + 48 + 20}{55}\right] \left[\frac{55 + 50}{100}\right] = .6 \times 2.33 \times 1.05 = 1.47$$

For the entire load:

$$11.09 + 10.24 + 7.53 + 1.47 = 30.33 \text{ units}$$

Following are the computations for a teacher of physics and algebra whose load is as follows:

a. Two sections of first-semester physics (with two double periods) with 24 and 26 eleventh-grade students.

b. Three classes in first-semester algebra, with 26, 24, and 28 ninth-grade students.

c. Three hours (four class periods) a week on the average throughout the semester spent in co-operations.

$PL = 45$ minutes.

For the physics classes:

$$1.1 \left[14 - \frac{11}{10} + \frac{350 - 350}{100}\right] \left[\frac{45 + 50}{100}\right] = 1.1 \ (14 - 1.1 + 0) \ (.95) = 13.48$$

For the algebra classes:

$$1.0 \left[15 - \frac{10}{10} + \frac{390 - 375}{100}\right] \left[\frac{45 + 50}{100}\right] = 1 \ (15 - 1 + .15) \ (.95) = 13.44$$

For co-operations:

$$.6 \times 4 \left[\frac{45 + 50}{100} \right] = .6 \times 4 \times .95 = 2.28$$

For the entire load:

$$13.48 + 13.44 + 2.28 = 29.20 \text{ units[7]}$$

Douglass and Rowe also developed norms for teaching load by subject field in the junior high school. The chart of these norms is represented by Figure 5.1.

Subject Field	Lower Quartile	Median	Upper Quartile
English	27.43	29.18	30.97
Art	25.39	27.37	30.00
Home Economics	25.60	27.33	29.26
Music	24.67	27.46	30.21
Mathematics	27.00	28.66	30.68
Industrial Arts	23.79	25.74	27.91
Physical Education	23.49	25.67	28.19
Commercial	26.64	28.97	30.55
Social Studies	27.37	29.31	31.18
Foreign Language	26.67	28.34	30.30
Science	27.74	29.50	31.54
Core Curriculum	27.00	29.28	31.54
Mixed Load	25.77	26.65	30.14
All Subjects	26.19	28.38	30.50

FIGURE 5.1. Tentative Norms of Teaching Load by Subject Field in the Junior High School.[8]

These figures are the actual compilation of total units in a work load from data forwarded by 2,656 teachers representing ninety-six junior high schools of Grades 7, 8 and 9.

NUMBER OF PERIODS AND LENGTH OF PERIODS

In recent years, there has been a trend toward a longer school day and, consequently, toward longer class periods at the sec-

---

[7]Douglass, pp. 82-83.
[8]Douglass, p. 85.

ondary level. The current norm is a seven-hour student day, including a lunch period of approximately thirty minutes. The longer periods provide the flexibility needed in instructional programs but also reduce the number of subjects a student may take during any one academic year. To compensate for this fact, some schools have added an *activity, zero,* or *early bird period* to allow students to take an additional elective or to participate in some activity.

Some schools utilize a *slip schedule* which provides two different beginning and ending times during the day. Students may come early and stay longer, adding an extra period in either the morning or afternoon, or they can follow a normal five- or six-period class schedule even though they begin and leave school at different times.

There has been a pronounced trend toward longer class periods and variation in the length of class periods, although limited research does not indicate significant differences with respect to increased achievement where the longer periods are used. McElhinny studied the relationship between length of class periods and academic achievement in 1960. Using matched pairs of ninth, tenth, and eleventh graders and the analysis of variance design, he concluded that although the test results were higher in a majority of the companions, none of the differences was significant at the 5 percent level of confidence.[9] However, studies including McElhinny's, found that teachers definitely favored the longer class periods (fifty-five minutes plus) over shorter ones (forty to forty-five minutes.)

The conventionally scheduled high school averages seven class periods of approximately fifty-five minutes in length, while the junior high schools have changed from eight or nine periods of forty or forty-five minutes to seven periods of approximately forty-eight to fifty minutes in length. A large enough number of schools are reporting varying lengths of class periods (sixty, seventy, ninety minutes) during the day to indicate a possible trend in this direction. Specific values of the lengthened class period as listed by Douglass include the following:

---

[9] J. Howard McElhinny, "The Length of the High School Class Period and Pupil Achievement" (Unpublished Ph.D. Dissertation, State University of Iowa, 1961), pp. 136-45.

1. Making each class a laboratory or a workshop rather than a recitation room.
2. Encouraging more thought in the "doing" subjects and more doing in the "thought" subjects.
3. Directing pupil growth and improving pupil behavior through increasing the time teachers spend with pupils and increasing the opportunities for observing pupils systematically.
4. Developing greater class interest and providing for individual difference through more differentiation of assignments.
5. Securing greater dividends on required homework by using more time in class to show pupils how to study.
6. Providing more favorable opportunity for class visitation to educational resources in the community.[10]

ROOM DETERMINATION AND
NUMBER OF TEACHING STATIONS

Rooms in a school building generally are classified into two major types of teaching stations: (1) *interchangeable stations* or nonspecial classrooms to be used by any conventional class (e.g., rooms for classes such as English or history); and (2) *special purpose stations* characterized by special equipment and space utilization requirements (e.g., rooms for such classes as agriculture, shop, and science laboratories). Determination of the number of students scheduled into these classes and the number of such rooms available relates directly to the Douglass scheduling process. Packer's formula is one means of computing the number of rooms needed for all classes.[11]

$$\text{Number of rooms} = \frac{\text{Registered Number of Pupils in a Subject}}{\text{Average size of Class}} \times \frac{\text{Average number of Periods Daily}}{\text{Number of periods in school day}}$$

Another means of determining the number of *interchangeable* stations needed is to use the following formula.[12]

---

[10]Douglass, p. 368.

[11]John H. Herrick; Ralph D. McLeary; Wilfred F. Clapp; and Walter F. Bogner, *From School Program to School Plant* (New York: Henry Holt and Company, 1956), pp. 115-16. Reprinted by permission of the publisher.

[12]Wallace H. Strevell, and Arvid Burke, *Administration of the School Building Program* (New York: McGraw-Hill Book Co., Inc., 1959), p. 153. Reprinted by permission of the publisher.

$$\text{Interchangeable Teacher Stations} = \frac{\dfrac{\text{Enrollment}}{8} + 12}{\text{Daily Periods}}$$

Example:

$$\begin{matrix}\text{400 Students} \\ \text{7 Daily Periods}\end{matrix} \quad \frac{\dfrac{400}{8} + 12}{7} = \frac{62}{9} = 9 \text{ stations needed}$$

In a surprisingly great number of cases, school principals fail to consider the common-sense factors related to room assignments. Some of these very basic nontechnical considerations are the following:

1. *Acoustical factors.* A class requiring relative quiet should not be scheduled near a shop, bandroom, or gymnasium.
2. *Size of rooms and relevance of the room to class scheduled.* Scheduling a class of forty-four for a room designed to hold thirty when there are other rooms available is inexcusable. Scheduling a class in creative writing in a room with no facilities for writing is another surprisingly common example of misassignment. Although these factors may be unavoidable in overcrowded schools, they do not exemplify administrative consideration in a normal school situation.

Principals not only should have a map or diagram of the campus on hand when assigning classrooms but also should keep an available room capacity and facilities chart designed similar to the example in Figure 5.2.

Room	Normal Capacity	Absolute Capacity	Facilities
142	44	52	Regular Student Desks
143	25	30	Tables and chairs no chalkboard

Figure 5.2. Room Facilities Work Chart

Access to such a chart provides considerable assistance to the administrator who is making room assignments during the construction of the Master Schedule.

3. *Location of rooms.* Students should be assigned to classrooms near facilities they need to use. For example, assigning a class for girls only to a room a great distance from a girls' rest room is not often considered the best example of room scheduling. Similarly, disabled youngsters should be located in areas of easy access to the central services and transportation.
4. *Room facilities and grade level or size of students.* The principal should be certain that furniture size is checked before making room assignments. Large six-foot senior boys do not fit well in furniture designed for junior-high youngsters.

GENERAL FACTORS TO
CONSIDER IN SCHEDULING

Additional factors which should be given specific consideration in developing the Master Schedule include the following:

1. *Age and physical disabilities of the teachers.* It is not prudent to schedule elderly or disabled teachers in classrooms that are up several flights of stairs or a long distance from the central office.
2. *Professional and academic preparation of the teacher.* The major and minor areas of concentration of the teachers should be the basis for class assignments. If the class is a "problem" class, experienced teachers often perform with more capability and confidence than a beginning teacher or one who has not had the previous professional or academic training and confidence needed to work with this particular group.
3. *Type of students.* If grouping is practiced in the school, certain teachers undoubtedly will prefer to work with either slow, average or fast youngsters. Whenever possible, teacher preference should be considered in these cases. Certain disciplinary problems should also be assigned to capable teachers.
4. *Teacher preference.* Many principals send a questionnaire to all teachers before assigning them to classes and

rooms. A summary of items found on several of these questionnaires includes:

a. Name, address, phone, etc.
b. Degree(s), major, minor.
c. Courses taught.
d. Preference of subjects: first and second choices, plus alternate choices.
e. Preference of ability group, plus alternate choices, if such grouping is used.
f. In a team situation, preference of subject area or teaching method, plus alternate choices.

PROCEDURES IN SCHEDULE CONSTRUCTION

Regardless of the grade level, certain procedural steps should be taken in constructing the Master Schedule. Some of these steps have been discussed previously and will only be listed here, but those specifically relevant to this unit are discussed in detail.

Constructing the Conventional Schedule. Basic procedures for constructing the conventional schedule are outlined and discussed below.

1. Determine policies and programs affecting total schedule construction.
2. Preregister and register students.
3. Obtain course enrollment figures and determine number of selections needed. List the courses offered, tally the registration cards, and then break down the total into sections.

    The total number of sections possible may be computed by multiplying the number of periods each faculty teaches by the number of faculty members. For example, if each faculty member is to teach five periods and there are seventeen faculty members, the total number of sections that can be offered is 17 X 5 or eighty-five sections. Fractional portions of periods can be computed separately and added in to the total. Thus, if three other faculty members are teaching three sections besides performing part-time administrative functions, these nine sections would be added to the total.

As a consequence, the sums of the breakdown of sections must equal the total number of sections the school can offer. In determining staff needs for the coming year, the principal simply computes the breakdown of sections as tallied and then asks for the necessary additional staff. It is apparent that the financial policy and ability of a given school district controls the class size to a great extent. An example of section determination follows in Figure 5.3.

Course	Tally	Totals	
		Students	Sections
English IV		80	3 or 4
Spanish IV		10	1
Journalism II		15	1
History IV		75	3
	Total Sections		8 or 9

FIGURE 5.3. Determining the Number of Sections

4. Assign Faculty. The size of the faculty and school directly control the number of different preparations a teacher must make. In smaller high schools, which have a maximum of 500 students, it is not unusual to find faculty who have three, four, and even five different preparations in four or more different subjects. Regardless of the size of faculty, some system or chart should be utilized to assign faculty to the various sections. The chart in Figure 5.4 illustrates one method of making these assignments.

5. Identify and eliminate conflicts. Although use of the conflict sheet was explained in Chapter Three, a brief review follows. Beginning with the cards for seniors, the principal checks each individual registration card for conflicts on a conflict sheet, mechanical key-sort device, or a special computer program for this purpose. These conflicts are tallied; priorities are established; and sections are placed

on the schedule board. Only single section classes need be plotted or checked for conflicts.

Other factors exist, however, which can create additional conflicts. Jacobson, Reavis and Logsdon have summarized research related to these factors.

Teacher	Assignment by Section	Sections	Total Sections
A	English III History II	2 3	5
B	Geometry I Counseling Office	3 2 (Equiv)	5
C	Boys Physical Education Hygiene	3 2	5

FIGURE 5.4. Teacher Assignment Sheet (Five Sections Maximum)

a. Adding a double period subject to a pupil's schedule will nearly always increase difficulties. Adding a single-period class to an individual program will not necessarily cause a greater number of conflicts.

b. There were almost 50 percent fewer conflicts in schools using the long period (55 or 60 minutes) with no double periods as against schools using short periods (40 or 45 minutes) with some subjects meeting for double periods.

c. Students who have irregular schedules, that is, who take subjects not ordinarily offered in their grade (probably because of previous failure), have many more conflicts per hundred students than a similar number of pupils whose elections are regular. For regular students scheduled in long periods (without double periods), the average number of conflicts was 0.013, but for the irregular students in the same schools under the same conditions, the average number of conflicts was 0.159, or twelve times as many conflicts per student.[13]

---

[13]Paul B. Jacobson, William C. Reavis, and James D. Logsdon, *The Effective School Principal*, 2d ed. (Englewood Cliffs, New Jersey: Prentice-Hall, Inc., 1963), p. 74. Reprinted by permission of the publisher.

The importance of having students list alternate choices during registration is clearly evident in the cases of students taking courses not usually included for their grade.

6. Construct the preliminary schedule. As was indicated earlier, numerous devices are utilized as schedule boards; no matter what the type used, however, it should provide for flexibility and allow the individual class section to be moved about the board freely. Some type of card or device should be constructed to represent each section (class offered), which might also indicate the number of students English IV A. (23)   If the course is for a specific grade level only, it might be color coded for easier identification. Beginning with the cards for senior classes, the principal first places the cards of the single sections on the workboard. Figure 5.5 illustrates a schedule board and the placement of single sections which might conflict.

Teacher	Advisory or Homeroom	1	2	3	Lunch	4	5	6
A			Engl. IV 24					
B				Hist. IV 30			Journ. 20	
C								

FIGURE 5.5. Placement of Conflict Courses on the Schedule.

In this particular instance, the school schedules a separate lunch hour. In other cases, however, several lunch periods are necessary and must be incorporated into the regular schedule. Details relating to lunch scheduling will be discussed later in this chapter.

If a *registration* schedule is used, class limits can be predetermined and students are able to register in the fall on a first-come, first-served basis. In most instances, however, such a document will be the foundation for the *master* schedule; consequently, the students will be placed arbitrarily into sections as they are scheduled. The philosophy of the school controls this procedure, and a policy decision must be made before registration begins.

After the single sections have been located on the schedule board, the remaining courses are plotted, utilizing the section and course assignment sheet developed earlier. The principal should keep in mind that too many teachers should not be scheduled for preparation or conference periods at the same time, as this situation means that a small number of faculty must account for a large number of students.

The work load or teacher load factors must constantly be kept in consideration. Although the final computation of teacher load is not made until the schedule is complete, a principal can balance several of the load factors while constructing the schedule.

			Room Assignment Schedule							
Room	Absolute Capacity	Desirable Capacity	Subject and Teacher by Periods							
1 2 3 4										

FIGURE 5.6. Room Assignment Schedule.

7. Assign rooms. After the preliminary schedule has been constructed, room assignments must be made. Ovard has illustrated a type of room assignment schedule which can be constructed to summarize the total utilization of the rooms by periods. This chart is depicted in Figure 5.6.[14]

8. Obtain faculty approval. When the preliminary schedule is completed, it should be posted and distributed to all

[14]Glen F. Ovard, *Administration of the Changing Secondary School* (New York: The Macmillan Company, 1966), p. 168. Copyright © 1966 by Glen F. Ovard. Reprinted by permission of the publisher and the author.

Western High School—Spring Semester 1968

Period	1	2	3	4	5	6	7
Start Finish	8:00 8:55	9:00 9:55	10:00 11:00	(class) 11:05 - 12:00 11:05 - 11:45 (lunch)	(lunch) 12:05 - 12:45 11:50 - 12:45 (class)	12:50 1:45	1:50 2:45
Science Biology I		Mrs. E. Lowery Phase 3 Room 502					
		Mr. L. Wilson Phase 2 Room 506					
Biology II	Mr. E. Hood Phase 3 Room 401		Mr. E. Hood Phase 3 Room 401		Mr. E. Hood Phase 3 Room 401	Mr. E. Hood Phase 3 Room 403	Mrs. E. Lowery Phase 3 Room 502
	Mrs. E. Lowery Phase 4 Room 502		Mrs. E. Lowery Phase 2 Room 502		Mr. G. Clark Phase 2 Room 403		
					Mrs. E. Lowery Phase 3 Room 502		
Advanced Biology AP	Block	Mr. G. Clark Phase 5 Block Room 403					
Advanced Biology II		Mr. E. Hood Phase 4 Room 401					

FIGURE 5.7. Registration Schedule. (Reprinted by courtesy of Western High School, Clark County School District, Las Vegas, Nevada.)

105

faculty members. Faculty suggestions should be discussed and the changes incorporated before a final Master Schedule is developed.

If the preliminary schedule is to be a Master Schedule for registration, it is more effective if the subject areas are placed in columns on the left, the periods are listed along the top, and the instructors names appear on cards in the squares. A portion of a *Registration Master Schedule* is illustrated in Figure 5.7.

The final *Master Schedule* follows the pattern recommended in Chapter Three. Figure 5.8 illustrates a portion of the same subject area as recorded in the final Master Schedule. Note that the faculty are listed in the left column and the subjects offered are now placed in the mosaic pattern.

SCHEDULING JUNIOR HIGH AND MIDDLE-SCHOOL PROGRAMS

The most common format used in scheduling at the junior-high or middle-school level is the block or group scheduling technique. The process can be manipulated either by hand or machine depending upon school policy. Generally, the block or group schedule is designed to allow one group of pupils to spend two or three consecutive periods under one teacher or a group of teachers. The steps in schedule construction vary somewhat depending upon whether the students preregister and are then arbitrarily assigned to a block or section or whether the blocks are predetermined and the students then register for a particular section (college system) until the class is filled. The organization of the curricular program and the type of program being used (ability-grouping, non-grading, conventional heterogenous classes, etc.) will control the policy decision in each instance. The fundamental steps for scheduling at the junior high school level follow:

Western High School
Class Schedule
Spring Semester 1968

Period	1	2	3	4	5	6	7
Start *Finish*	*8:00* *8:55*	*9:00* *9:55*	*10:00* *11:00*	*(class)* *11:05 - 12:00* *11:05 - 11:45* *(lunch)*	*(lunch)* *12:05 - 12:45* *11:50 - 12:45* *(class)*	*12:50* *1:45*	*1:50* *2:45*
Science							
56. Mr. E. Hood	Biology II Phase 3, 401	Adv. Biology II Phase 4, 401	Biology II Phase 3, 401	Lunch	Biology II Phase 3, 401	Biology II Phase 3, 401	Conference
57. Mr. G. Clark	Adv. Biology AP Phase 5, 403		Physiology II Phase 4, 403	Lunch	Biology II Phase 2, 403	Physiology I Phase 4, 403	Conference
58. Mrs. E. Lowery	Biology II Phase 4, 502	Biology I Phase 3, 502	Biology II Phase 2, 502	Lunch	Biology II Phase 3, 502	Conference	Biology II Phase 3, 502
59. Mr. L. Wilson	Photography II Phase 4, 506	Biology I Phase 2, 506	Photography I Phase 3, 506	Lunch	Conference	Photography I Phase 3, 506	Photography I Phase 3, 506
60. Miss M. Shark	Chemistry II Phase 3, 405	Chemistry II Phase 5, 405	Chemistry II Phase 4, 405	Lunch	Chemistry II Phase 3, 405	Chemistry II Phase 4, 405	Conference
61. Mr. L. Casey	Physics II Phase 4, 504	Chemistry I Phase 3-4, 504	Physics II Phase 3, 504	Lunch	Physics I Phase 4, 504	Conference	Physical Science I Phase 3, 504
62. Mr. Tom Daly	Conference	Biology II Phase 3, 502	Biology II Phase 2, 401	Lunch	Biology II Phase 3, 403	Quest Lab Supervisor	Quest Lab Supervisor
Home Economics							
63. Mrs. M. McClincy	Conference	Special Clothing Phase 3-5, 118	Clothing II Phase 3-5, 118	Clothing II Phase 305, 118	Lunch	Clothing II Phase 3-5, 118	Clothing I Phase 1-5, 118

FIGURE 5.8. Master Schedule of Courses Illustrated in Figure 5.7. (Reprinted by courtesy of Western High School, Clark County School District, Las Vegas, Nevada.)

1. Register all students using either conventional color coded cards, IBM mark-sense cards, or marginal key punch cards.
2. Determine the number of sections needed for each subject. Then arrange all required courses into a pattern using the time periods and block or group sections. The following chart illustrates such an arrangement for four groups of twenty-five students each in three required and one elective classes at the eighth-grade level (Figure 5.9). If only one elective is permitted, a specific period might be set aside for this elective for either the boys or girls, or for both, depending upon the elective taken.

Class	Group I Period	Group II	Group III	Group IV
English 8	1	2	3	4
History 8	4	5	6	7
Science 8	7	1	2	3
Elective	3	4	5	6

FIGURE 5.9. Assigning the Number of Block Sections.

3. Consider possible conflicts. Generally, a conflict chart is not necessary, since most of the courses are required and the number of sections easily determined. However, if approximately one-half of the program is composed of electives, then a conflict sheet could be used to schedule around the predetermined blocks. The back-to-back scheduling factor discussed in Chapter Six also would require some maneuvering of class cards on the schedule board.
4. Construct the schedule by using a board similar to the one considered in the discussion of the mosaic plan and develop an outline by placing the names of the faculty vertically on the left, the time periods horizontally at the top, and the various classes in the squares.

Grade	60 Min.	60 Min.	60 Min.	40 Min.	60 Min.	60 Min.	60 Min.
7	Core			L U N C H	Exploratory	Math	Physical Education
8	Core		Exploratory	L U N C H	Exploratory	Math	Physical Education
9	Core	Exploratory	Exploratory	L U N C H	Elective	Math Elective	Physical Education

FIGURE 5.10. Suggested Time Allotment for Junior High School Program by Grades.[15]

---

[15]Nelson L. Bossing and Roscoe V. Cramer, *The Junior High School* (Boston: Houghton Mifflin Company, 1966), p. 174. Reprinted by permission of the publisher and of James M. Phillips.

5. Complete the Master Schedule. After completion, all data should be printed and distributed to the appropriate personnel.

Bossing and Cramer illustrate their recommendation for probable time allotment in a junior high school which uses a core program and block-time schedule. This chart is depicted in Figure 5.10.

A similar schedule pattern would be adaptable to the numerous middle schools springing up throughout the nation.

OTHER SCHEDULING FACTORS

Lunch Hours. Secondary schools operating with one lunch hour and a cafeteria large enough to accommodate the total student body have little concern with lunchroom conflicts. Larger schools, however, may require that three or more lunch periods be incorporated into the regular schedule because of a limited dining area. In some cases, these facilities are designed for multiple lunch scheduling.

Period		*Period*	
1	8:00 8:55	5	11:35 12:30
2	9:00 9:55	6	12:35 1:30
3	10:00 10:55	7	1:35 2:30
4 (Lunch)	11:00 11:30		

FIGURE 5.11. A Single Lunch Period Schedule in a School with Fifty-five Minute Periods.

A single period lunch schedule in a school with six class periods and a seventh period lunch assignment would appear something like the schedule in Figure 5.11.

The lunch period may or may not be counted as a numbered period. If it is not directly associated with an activity or intramural schedule, it normally runs for thirty to forty minutes; when activities are scheduled during the noon hour, the regular or even extended period is used.

In cases where more than one lunch period is necessary, various means have been utilized to schedule students. For example, if two lunch periods are needed for a fifty-five minute period schedule, the lunch hour could count as a regular class and the youngsters could be scheduled in equal numbers into two convenient periods. Figure 5.12 presents an example of this approach.

Period 3	Period 4 Class or Lunch	Period 5 Class or Lunch	Period 6
10:00	11:00	12:00	1:00
10:55	11:55	12:55	1:55

FIGURE 5.12. A Two Lunch Hour Schedule.

If the two lunch periods are shortened, the two concurrent lunch schedules can be varied and integrated as the illustration in Figure 5.   shows.

Period 4		Period 5	
Class	11:05 — 12:00	Lunch	12:05 — 12:45
Lunch	11:05 — 11:45	Class	11:50 — 12:45

FIGURE 5.13 Two Shortened Integrated Lunch Periods.

A three-wave lunch hour could be divided into three units within a two- or three-period time phase. At times, however, these can become quite complex and force students to split a class period. For example, Figure 5.14 outlines a three-phase, split lunch schedule.

	Period 4	11:00 11:55	12:00 12:55	Period 5
Student A	Lunch A		Class A	Class A
Student B	Class B		Lunch	Class B

FIGURE 5.14. A Three-Phase Split Lunch Schedule.

Maxey has described a five-wave schedule designed for a large Seattle high school. This schedule follows in Figure 5.15.

Lunch Schedule		4th-Period Class Groups	
1st lunch	11:40 - 12:10	12:10	1:10
2nd lunch	11:55 - 12:25	11:40 - 11:55	12:25 - 1:10
3rd lunch	12:10 - 12:40	11:40 - 12:10	12:40 - 1:10
4th lunch	12:25 - 12:55	11:40 - 12:25	12:55 - 1:10
5th lunch	12:40 - 1:10	11:40	12:40

1st lunch — 30 minutes and then to class for 55 minutes
2nd lunch — to class for 15 minutes; to lunch for 30 minutes
and to class for 45 minutes
3rd lunch — to class for 30 minutes; to lunch for 30 minutes
and then to class for 30 minutes
4th lunch — to class for 45 minutes; to lunch for 30 minutes
and back to class for 15 minutes
5th lunch — to class for 55 minutes; then to lunch for 30 minutes

FIGURE 5.15. A Five-Wave Lunch Schedule.[16]

Assembly Schedules and Activity Schedules. Even after the time units have been assigned to the regular daily schedule, other school programs often affect this established pattern. If an assembly period, activity period, or even an additional regular length time period is included on a weekly or monthly basis, some provision must be made for this change. Numerous devices have been tried to solve this problem, and many have

[16]John C. Maxey, "A New Idea on Lunch Period Scheduling—The Five-Wave Plan," *Bulletin of NASSP* 46 (April 1962): 43-50.

proved effective. Their effectiveness, however, closely relates to the individual school program and the methods used to construct the total schedule. A copy of the revised schedule should be a part of the Master Schedule and available to all students and faculty.

Some of the means employed to adjust for these special activities are briefly discussed in the following paragraphs.

Rotating Schedule. This type of schedule may be used to vary the length of periods or to rotate an assembly, activity or homeroom period. An example of each case is illustrated in Figures 5.16 and 5.17.

Regular	1st week assembly	2nd week assembly
Monday (noon)	Tues. (assembly)	Tues. (assembly)
1	1	2
2	2	3
3	assembly 10 a.m.	assembly 10 a.m.
4	4	4
5	5	6
6	6	1

Figure 5.16. A Single Day Rotation Schedule (Assembly).

Period	1	2	3	4	5	6
Monday	A	B	C	D	E	F
Tuesday	D	E	F	A	B	C
Wednesday	B	C	D	E	F	A
Thursday	E	F	A	B	C	D
Friday	C	D	E	F	A	B

Figure 5.17. Rotation Schedule of All Periods.

The purpose of the rotation schedule in Figure 5.17 is to avoid the monopolization of key time periods by one or two classes during the morning. An attempt is made to give all periods some opportunity to meet before noon during "prime time." There is no evidence to suggest that this type of schedule provides the gains sought; in fact, the confusion resulting from such a process possibly outweighs the positive factor gained from conducting classes during prime time.

Another example of a rotation schedule designed to vary the time during which courses are offered is depicted in Figure 5.18.

Time	Mon.	Tues.	Wed.	Thurs.	Fri.
30 min.	1	2	3	4	5
80 min.	2	3	4	5	6
50 min.	3	4	5	6	1
70 min.	4	5	6	1	2
30 min.	5	6	1	2	3
110 min.	6	1	2	3	4

FIGURE 5.18.   Rotation Schedule with Time Variation.

Floating Period Schedule.   If any activity course, such as physical education, is required and the schedule of six periods restricts electives, a *floating period* schedule may be utilized to vary the subject offered and permit an additional elective. The following schedule (Figure 5.19) was adapted from a pattern employed in the Palo Alto, California, Unified School District and reprinted by Jack Rand in a school district brochure. Physical education is the "floating" class.

Period	Mon.	Tues.	Wed.	Thurs.	Fri.
1	Eng.	Eng.	Eng.	Eng.	P.E.
2	P.E.	Geom.	Geom.	Geom.	Geom.
3	Hist.	Hist.	P.E.	Hist.	Hist.
4	Elective	P.E.	Elective	Elective	Elective

FIGURE 5.19.   The Floating Period: Physical Education.

The Minimum Day Schedule.   In some cases principals have the legal authority to establish *minimum days,* days when students are released early while the faculty members remain for special sessions, curricular meetings, etc. In some special situation, schools are closed on minimum days. The normal scheduling procedure for minimum days is to subtract five to ten minutes from each period and add it to the end of the day. Thus, a seven-period day (fifty-five minute periods) could have eight minutes subtracted from each period, and school would then be released fifty-five or fifty-six minutes earlier. Larger amounts of time can be subtracted if more released time is needed. The minimum day schedule should be tabulated and posted for all to use. An example of such a schedule follows in Figure 5.20.

Regular Schedule		Minimum Day Schedule (Minimum 55 minutes)	
1	8:00 — 8:55	1	8:00 — 8:47
2	9:00 — 9:55	2	8:52 — 9:35
3	10:00 — 10:55	3	9:40 — 10:23
4	11:00 — 11:55	4	10:28 — 11:09
5	12:00 — 12:55	5	11:14 — 11:57
6	1:00 — 1:55	6	12:02 — 12:45
7	2:00 — 2:55	7	12:50 — 1:32

FIGURE 5.20. Minimum Day Schedule.

Adjustments for lunch will need to be considered in a minimum day schedule. If a full afternoon is scheduled, the lunch plan should be included. In some cases, however, minimum days are planned to terminate at noon and release the students for lunch time, freeing the school from this responsibility on that particular day.

DOUBLE SESSIONS: EXTENDING THE SCHOOL DAY

When schools become overcrowded they generally are forced to move either to double sessions or year-round operations. To achieve this end, class periods are added, and the class period itself is shortened to produce double sessions for two student waves. The number of periods added should correlate with the number of additional sections added. Usually, one of two techniques or variations of these techniques is utilized. In one plan, the school establishes two school days or sessions, utilizing forty to forty-five minute periods. Students are scheduled totally in Session I or Session II and attend class on this basis.

Session I	*Session II*
8:00 – 12:20	12:20 – 4:40
Periods 1-7 (forty minutes)	Periods 1-7 (forty minutes) or 8-14

In the other plan, the school day is extended by adding the necessary number of periods to absorb the sections needed. The school day remains continuous and students attend on the basis of a college-format, leaving campus after a class is finished. An example of a student's schedule under this plan follows:

Student A

Period	1	2	3	4	5	6	7	8	9	10	11	12
Class	Eng.		Hist.			Math	P.E.	Fr.	Sci.			

(40-45 minute periods)

FIGURE 5.21.

The pattern employed depends upon several conditions affecting the local school district. Transportation schedules, urban or rural location, the faculty available—all of these factors determine the type of schedule utilized. It could well be that different schools in the same district might use different scheduling patterns because of different factors in individual situations.

Ovard has identified other means which schools have employed in scheduling for excess students. These practices are listed below.

Overload the Building Facilities. Through the use of portable seats, all available space within the classroom is used for student seating. Such a practice decreases the functional use of the room for nearly all activities but lecture and discussion. Cafeterias, auditoriums, music rooms, and all special facilities are used whenever possible.

Double Sessions. Another solution is to have double sessions. One half of the students go to school from 8 to 12 A.M. and the other half attend from 12 to 4 P.M. The facilities thus accommodate double the normal amount. Class periods are frequently shortened to 40 minutes. All studying is done at home. Among the problems presented by this plan are: students receive little supervised study, bus transportation is more complicated, students have too much free time, teachers must work extra hours or share facilities with a whole new administration and teaching staff, and time for proper custodial care is reduced.

Extended School Day. Some school principals solve the excess-number-of-students problem by extending the school day. School classes start earlier and go later. The number of periods is increased from six or seven to 10 or 11. Some students start as early as seven o'clock in the morning, and leave by one, two or three o'clock in the afternoon. Others arrive at later hours but stay in school until five or six o'clock in the evening. The lunch schedule extends over several periods. Homeroom and activity periods are planned in the morning and afternoon so all students can be involved. Some disadvantages of this type of schedule involve bus transportation, supervision of students throughout activity and lunch periods while other classes are in session, and assignment of teachers. Both the administrative personnel and the teachers can be "worked to death" unless clear-cut policies regarding load and assignment are followed.

Platoon System. Another method is to block students into sections or platoons. This method was discussed under the block method of scheduling. Students are blocked in activity classes, as well as required subjects. Creative activity blocks alternate with content blocks. Some schools report that this plan can increase the facilities up to one quarter of the capacity.

Multiple Load and Balance. Under a "multiple load and balance" plan all available space is used except the visual-aid room and the cafeteria. The over-all capacity of the building is determined by the following computation: The library is to house 10 per cent of its capacity, the physical education class is to be held at 55 students, home economics and shops are to be held to their statutory limits, and the classroom is to be computed at 30 X number of rooms X 1.2. Classes are arranged for library experiences. By planning to send four classes into the library for planned experience, extending the school day by one period, and using the building to capacity, the school capacity may be increased by 35 per cent.[17]

QUESTIONS AND SUGGESTIONS FOR STUDY

1. Why is the establishment of policies regarding the school program so important to schedule construction?

2. Of what value is the school schedule?

3. How can a principal estimate the number of sections and staff he will need?

4. Of what specific value is a conflict sheet?

5. Define the areas of procedure in schedule construction which are common to conventional, machine, and marginal scheduling.

6. How might a school district schedule for overloads or excess students?

7. How do the mosaic and block schedules differ?

8. Why is the computer potentially so valuable to the school principal for use in schedule construction?

9. Develop a list of criteria for a good secondary school schedule.

10. Why is junior-high or middle-school scheduling generally simpler than senior high school schedule building?

11. Conduct a survey of the teachers in your area to determine their preferences with respect to: a. number of preparations, b. length of class period, and c. participation in policy decision related to scheduling.

12. Examine fifteen or twenty schedules from high schools in your general area or from different portions of the state. Identify and list areas in which they differ.

---

[17]Ovard, Glen F., pp. 173-174.

Scheduling Assignments

Valley Senior High School

School Enrollment:	320 (Grades 10-12)
Number of Teachers:	12
Number of Class Periods:	6
Number of Sections per Teacher:	5
Length of Class Periods:	55 minutes

School Offerings and Enrollment

Subject	*Enrollment*	*No. Sections*
English IV	98	_____
English III	103	_____
English II	100	_____
Debate	16	_____
Journalism	22	_____
Modern Problems	98	_____
American History	102	_____
World History	100	_____
Metal Work	20	_____
Mechanical Drawing	25	_____
Woodwork III	21	_____
Woodwork II	41	_____
Home Economics III	16	_____
Home Economics II	20	_____
Bookkeeping	29	_____
Typing II	28	_____
Typing I	63	_____
Shorthand II	16	_____
Shorthand I	33	_____
Trigonometry	28	_____
Adv. Algebra	50	_____
Geometry	97	_____
Chemistry	30	_____
Physics	48	_____
Biology	100	_____
Spanish IV	15	_____
Spanish III	30	_____
Spanish II	60	_____
Girls' Vocal Music	50	_____

Subject	Enrollment	No. Sections
Boys' Vocal Music	40	_____
Choir	66	_____
Band	55	_____
Girls' Phys. Ed.	150	_____
Boys' Phys. Ed.	150	_____

Total Sections _____

Scheduling Assignment
Individual Student Class Program

Seniors	Juniors	Sophomores
English IV A Modern Problems Physical Education (Boys) Journalism Chemistry Trigonometry	English III H American History Physical Education (Boys) Physics Advanced Algebra Debate	English II O World History Physical Education (Girls) Biology Spanish II Home Economics II
English IV B Modern Problems Physical Education (Girls) Shorthand II Typing II Girls' Vocal	English III I American History Physical Education (Boys) Woodwork II Metal Work Mechanical Drawing	English II P Biology Geometry Physical Education (Boys) Boys' Vocal Typing I
English IV C Modern Problems Physical Education (Girls) Debate Trigonometry Band	English III J American History Physical Education (Girls) Debate Shorthand I Choir	English II Q Biology Geometry Physical Education (Boys) Woodwork II Band
English IV D Modern Problems Physical Education (Girls) Bookkeeping Typing II Shorthand II	English III K American History Physical Education (Girls) Spanish III Band Advanced Algebra	English II R Biology Geometry Physical Education (Girls) Typing I Choir
English IV E Modern Problems Physical Education (Boys) Chemistry Trigonometry Mechanical Drawing	English III L American History Physical Education (Boys) Geometry Woodwork III Mechanical Drawing	English II S Biology World History Physical Education (Boys) Mechanical Drawing Metal Work
English IV F Modern Problems Physical Education (Boys) Spanish IV Physics Band	English III M American History Physical Education (Girls) Geometry Home Economics III Choir	English II T Biology World History Physical Education (Girls) Girls' Vocal Band
English IV G Modern Problems Physical Education (Boys) Debate Journalism Spanish IV	English III N American History Physical Education (Boys) Debate Spanish III Band	English II U Biology World History Physical Education (Boys) Spanish II Choir

1. All teachers have one conference period.
2. There is only one gymnasium with no partitions.

13. Survey a selected number of high schools to determine how they compute teacher load. What different techniques do they use?

14. Construct a conventional schedule following the procedures outlined in this chapter and using the information on the following pages. Second, construct a similar schedule using marginal key-sort tools and data processing, if either is available.

SELECTED REFERENCES

Anderson, G. Ernst. "How to Schedule with a Computer." *Nation's Schools* (April 1965): 80-82.

Anderson, Lester W., and Van Dyke, Lauren A. *Secondary School Administration.* Boston: Houghton Mifflin Company, 1963, Chapter 6, "Organizations of the School Schedule and Calendar."

Austin, David B.; French, Will; and Hull, J. Dan. *American High School Administration.* New York: Holt, Rinehart, and Winston, 1962, Chapter 12, "Schedule-Making and School Organization."

Bent, Rudyard K., and McCann, Lloyd E. *Administration of Secondary Schools.* New York: McGraw-Hill Book Co., 1960., Chapter 12, "Coordinating the School Program."

Bossing, Nelson L., and Cramer, Roscoe V. *The Junior High School.* Boston: Houghton Mifflin Company, 1966, Chapters 6 and 7, "Block-Time Class Organization" and "The Core Curriculum."

Brown, Frank. *The Nongraded High School.* Englewood Cliffs, New Jersey: Prentice-Hall, 1963, Chapter 8, "A Change of Pace."

Bulletin of the NASSP 43 (January 1960). Entire Issue.

Bulletin of the NASSP 44 (January 1961). Entire Issue.

Bulletin of the NASSP 45 (January 1962). Entire Issue.

Bush, Robert N. "Decision for the Principal: Hand or Computer Scheduling." *Bulletin of the NASSP* 48 (April 1964).

Douglass, Harl R. Modern Administration of the Secondary Schools, 2d ed. Boston: Ginn and Company, 1963, Chapters 5 and 16, "Arranging Staff Assignments" and "Constructing the Schedule."

Jacobson, Paul B.; Reavis, William C.; and Logsdon, James D. *The Effective School Principal,* 2d ed. Englewood Cliffs, New Jersey: Prentice-Hall, 1963, Chapter 4, "Making a School Schedule."

Jung, Christian A. "Revision of the Douglass Teaching Load Formula." Unpublished Ed.D. dissertation, University of Colorado, 1950.

Linder, Ivan H., and Gunn, Henry M. *Secondary School Administration: Problems and Practices.* Columbus, Ohio: Charles E. Merrill Publishing Co., 1963, Chapter 11, "Schedule Construction and Registration."

Manlove, Donald C., and Beggs, David W. III. *Flexible Scheduling.* Bloomington, Indiana: Indiana University Press, 1966.

Maxey, John C. "A New Idea on Lunch Period Scheduling—The Five-Wave Plan." *Bulletin of the NASSP* 46 (April 1962).

McElhinny, J. Howard. "The Length of the High School Class Period and Pupil Achievement." Unpublished Ph.D. dissertation, State University of Iowa, 1961.

National Education Association. *The American School Teacher.* Research Monograph MZ. Washington, D.C.: National Education Association, April, 1963.

Ovard, Glen F. *Administration of the Changing Secondary School.* New York: The Macmillan Co., 1966, Chapter 7, "Schedule-Making."

School Scheduling by Computer—The Story of GASP. New York: Educational Facilities Laboratories, Inc., 1964.

Trump, J. Lloyd. *Images of the Future.* Commission on the Experimental Study of the Utilization of the Staff in the Secondary School, 1959.

Chapter Six

Flexible Programming and Computer-Based Approaches

The development of various flexible, performance-oriented programs and the mechanization of scheduling has required a refocus of the traditional procedures used in schedule construction. The marginal Key-Sort Kits, a form of mechanical machine scheduling, are giving way to sophisticated electronic computer-based instructional programming. The various types of flexible schedules and innovative processes and machines used in instructional programming will be reviewed in greater detail in this chapter.

REGISTRATION

Computer-based scheduling permits a closer tie-in between the registration process and schedule construction. The electronic computer is a device that demands a set of carefully prepared instructions called the *computer program* (or *software*) to carry out its rapid operations. The key element for registration and scheduling of instructional activities is, therefore, the computer program.[1]

---

[1]"Stanford School Scheduling System" (SSSS) at Valley High and Rancho High Schools, Clark County School District, Las Vegas, Nevada.

123

A Computer Coordinated, Team Teaching, Modular Program.
The preregistration procedure in this approach would include
the following:

1. In January, the various departments or faculty teams meet
   to review the course of study and current organizational
   procedures and to revise the curriculum offerings in the
   Registration Guide. The *Guide* is then sent to all parents
   via the student for study and planning.
2. Students are preregistered during grade card distribution. Two IBM mark-sense (X-61) cards with the student's
   name and number are used to collect certain types of data.
   These cards are then key punched and serve as input
   sources to two computers which, in turn, print out two
   preregistration cards. The student records his primary
   requests on one card and his secondary or alternate
   choices on the other. All courses have code numbers and
   the student simply marks the code number for the appropriate area.

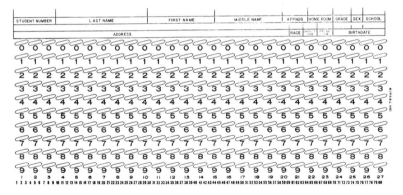

FIGURE 6.1. Sample Computer-based Preregistration
Card before Being Marked by the Student. (Reprinted
by courtesy of Valley High School, Clark County
School District, Las Vegas, Nevada.)

The first course entered on the card receives priority consideration. A sample card is pictured in Figure 6.1. Cards
also are sometimes color coded to distinguish class or
grade levels. Figure 6.2 represents a coded course request
form used by students to select classes they prefer.

1968-69 School Year

Name _____
Last,   First   Initial

Circle your primary course requests. Place a check mark by each alternate. The alternate should be for the same number of credits as the primary course request. Be sure that you are familiar with the registration requirements and the various course prerequisites.

Place the code number of your primary course request in the first column. You should choose an alternate for each elective. Place the code number of the alternate course in the second column directly opposite the original choice. Please list your primary course requests in order of preference. This will establish a priority for building the schedule.

Priority No.	Primary Request	Alternate	Credits
1			
2			
3			
4			
5			
6			
7			1
		Total Credits	

Code	Course	Code	Course	Code	Course	Code	Course	Code	Course
121	English A1	191	German I	362	Shhd 2/Tran	600	I A Survey*	704	Fab Design
122	English A2	192	German II	365	Cl Off Pra	601	Auto I	705	Drwg WC
131	English B1	193	German III	371	Bkkpg I	602	Auto II	706	Painting
132	English B2	194	German IV	374	Steno Prac	603	Auto Serv	707	Comm Dsgn
141	English C1	201	Am History	375	Bus Math	604	Sp Prob Au	708	Graphics
142	English C2	202	Am Govt	376	Bus Engl	611	Metal I	800	Vars Band
144	Adv Comp	203	Gphy A	377	Bus Law	612	Metal II	801	Int Band
150	Beg Drama*	204	Gphy B	381	Marketing	613	Sp Prob Me	802	Beg Band*
151	Adv Drama*	205	Gphy C	382	Dist Ed	621	Wood I	803	Orchestra*
152	Beg Speech*	210	Psychology	384	Con Econ	622	Wood II	804	Stage Band*
153	Adv Speech*	212	Sociology	400	Physics	623	Sp Prob Wd	810	A Cappella
155	Debate	215	Human Relat	402	Chemistry	630	Gen Elect	811	Girls Glee*
160	Humanities*	300	Appld Math	404	Biology	631	Elect I	812	Boys Chor*
162	Journalism*	301	Algebra I	405	Bio Pat+Pr	632	Elect II	813	Music Thry
164	Publictns*	305	Geometry	410	Sci Pat+Pr	635	Elect Main*	814	Madrigals
171	French I	312	Algebra II	412	Adv Sci	638	Home Main*	815	Folk Sing*
172	French II	315	Tri Fun	501	Hmkg I	641	Draft I	900	Boys P.E.*
174	French III	320	Sen Math	502	Bach Arts*	642	Draft II	922	Girls P.E.*
174	French IV	330	Comp Sci*	512	Hmkg II	643	Draft III	940	Health
181	Spanish I	331	Comp Sem	513	Cloth Con	644	Arch Draw	950	Driver Ed)*
182	Spanish II	350	Pers Type	514	Adv Foods	700	Vis Comm*		
183	Spanish III	351	Typing I	515	H H Furn	701	Beg Design*		
184	Spanish IV	352	Typing II	516	Fam Living	702	Sculpture		
185	Conv Span*	361	Shrthnd I	517	Sp Prob Hm	703	Ceramics		

*One-half credit course

All Juniors must enroll in: English, American History and P.E. All Seniors must enroll in: English and American Govt.

FIGURE 6.2. A Coded Course Request Form. (Reproduced by courtesy of Clark County Schools, Las Vegas, Nevada.)

125

3. These cards are collected in the homeroom and forwarded to the staff member responsible for the scheduling
process. After the cards are read and punched by machine, a print-out containing a count of all code numbers
and course titles is made (see Figure 6.3).

404	427	Biology
405	138	Bio Pat and PR
410	055	Sci Pat and PR
412	023	Adv Sci
501	028	Hmkg I
502	113	Bach Arts
512	056	Hmkg II

FIGURE 6.3. Portion of Print-Out Sheet Containing
Course Enrollments.

4. The print-out sheet is sent to the faculty teams by department chairmen who project their total enrollment figures
and determine staffing needs before forwarding this information to the principal. The principal then contacts the
Central Personnel Office and negotiates staff needs based
on these projections.
5. The faculty (by teams or departments) now begins the
process of developing a course "structure." At this time,
the number of teachers, number of students in each class,
and the number of classes have been determined. The
structuring process involves consideration of the total
time in class, the number of phases (large groups, small
groups, lab groups), and how such elements as the
modules of thirty minutes each are to be calculated into
weekly cycles.
6. Each department then forwards its information to the
schedule coordinator who in turn compiles the information on a Consolidated Structure Sheet (see Figure 6.4).
7. The data on the completed information sheet now must
be converted into computer input or IBM cards. These
punched cards are fed into a computer programmed to

Structure Sheet

| | A | B | C | D | E* | F | G | H | First Teacher | | | Second Teacher | | | Third Teacher | | | First Choice | Alternate |
									I	J	K**	I₁	J₁	K₁	I₂	J₂	K₂	L	M
	Course Code	Course Name (10)	P P M	P M W		NT	T/S	# Sec.	Teacher (12)	# Sec.		Teacher (12)	# SEC.		Teacher (12)	# Sec.		Room Number (3)	Room Number (3)
Phase 1																			
Phase 2	//////	//////																	
Phase 3	//////	//////																	
Phase 4	//////	//////																	

E Total _____
Day Independence _____
 Phase 1 _____
 Phase 2 _____

K Total _____
 Phase 3 _____
 Phase 4 _____

K₁ Total _____
K₂ Total _____

*E is computed by (C times D)
**K is computed by (E times J)

E.S.S. _____
T.V. _____

Department Coordinator _____ (initial)

FIGURE 6.4. Consolidation Structure Sheet. (Reprinted by courtesy of Valley High School, Clark County School District, Las Vegas, Nevada.)

organize the data in the cards into a schedule. It should be noted that the information on the original preregistration card must be transferred to a different IBM card before being forwarded to the computer. Three sets of cards per student are actually included, while all correction cards and late enrollment cards are compiled and forwarded later.

College-Type, Nongraded, Semester Programs.[2]   A two-semester program may be utilized by some schools. In such a program, each semester is treated as an entity in itself. Courses do not necessarily continue throughout the year, and, as a consequence, the student frequently needs to change his program for the semester. A separate preregistration and registration period is scheduled each semester.

When the total high school program is nongraded, or in a *continuous progress mode,* students registering for the different phases on the basis of advisement and interest will follow a different set of procedures. The procedure is as follows and will be illustrated with Keysort rather than computer cards.

1. Preregistration takes place in November and March.
2. The students receive the combination student handbook and course catalog in advance and are encouraged to take this material home. During a specified two- or three-week period, students meet with homeroom teachers and counselors to discuss their programs.
3. Each student develops a Student Plan Sheet and completes *two preregistration cards using the Plan Sheet as a guide.* One registration card is received by the counselor, and the other is taken home for a parent's signature of approval. The student's preregistration is not completed until he has returned the reregistration card signed by the parent. Figure 6.5 illustrates a portion of the Plan Sheet used to develop the student's request for courses.
4. Students record their programs for the coming semester on a card similar to that illustrated in Figure 6.6. The front

---

[2]Western High School, Clark County School District, Las Vegas, Nevada.

Class Schedule

Period	Subject	Teacher	Room Number
1. — (class) (enrichment) Begins 8:00 a.m. Ends 8:55 a.m.			
2. — (class) (busses arrive at 8:50 a.m.) Begins 9:00 a.m. Ends 10:00 a.m.			
3. — (class) (homeroom period) Begins 10:00 a.m. Ends 11:00 a.m.			
4. — (class) Begins 11:05 a.m. Ends 11:45 a.m.			

FIGURE 6.5. Portion of Student Plan Sheet.

section contains student *preregistration requests,* while the back is used for *final registration* during the first day of the semester. If a student is taking six subjects, he must list two alternate choices; if he takes five subjects, he is required to list three alternate subjects on this card.

A suggested course sequence is described in the catalog for each subject area. An example of recommended course sequence for bookkeeping is illustrated in Figure 6.7.

5. A Master Schedule is developed from the student requests by the assistant principal assigned this responsibility. Mas-

STUDENT'S NAME _____
PRINT LAST _____ FIRST _____ MIDDLE _____ NICKNAME _____ GRADE _____

ADDRESS _____ BIRTHDATE _____ AGE _____
(month - day - year of birth)

CITY _____ ZIP CODE _____ HOME PHONE _____ SEX ___ M ___ F RACE _____

EMERGENCY PHONE _____ EMERGENCY NAME _____

FATHER'S NAME _____ EMPLOYM'T _____ PHONE _____

MOTHER'S NAME _____ EMPLOYM'T _____ PHONE _____

REGISTRATION DATE _____ TYPE E _____ R _____ WITHDRAWAL DATE _____ TYPE W _____

WITHDRAWAL APPROVAL BY _____ DESTINATION _____

FIRST SEMESTER

PER	COURSE	TEACHER	ROOM
1			
2			
3			
4			
5 LUNCH			
6			
7			

SECOND SEMESTER

PER	COURSE	TEACHER	ROOM
1			
2			
3			
4			
5 LUNCH			
6			
7			

FIGURE 6.6. Keysort Preregistration Card. (Reprinted by courtesy of Western High School, Clark County School District, Las Vegas, Nevada.)

Interest Area	Sequence	Additional Electives
Bookkeeping	General Business Business Mathematics	Shorthand I Shorthand II
	Bookkeeping I Typing I	Typing II Business Law
	Bookkeeping II Business English ½ credit	

FIGURE 6.7. Suggested Course Sequence for Bookkeeping. (Reprinted by courtesy of Western High School, Clark County School District, Las Vegas, Nevada.)

ter Schedules completed after spring preregistration are mailed to the student's home during the summer for study and review.

6. Students register between semesters and at the beginning of the school year using the reverse side of the preregistration card (see Figure 6.8).

Mass registration occurs in the gymnasium over a period of a day and one-half. Teachers are located at tables by departments so that students can register for their requested courses by subject area. A tally sheet is manned at each table as students sign up for classes. One copy of the tally sheet goes to the instructor, while the other is forwarded to the office.

Other Registration Procedures. Secondary schools across the nation utilize numerous variations of the registration procedures discussed in the preceding paragraphs. It is important to note that, to a great extent, the type of scheduling pattern and the organization of the curriculum and instructional program determine a school's registration pattern. For example, the nongraded high school plan initiated in Melbourne, Florida, uses some very unusual procedures for registration. B. Frank Brown

REGISTRATION CARD

LAST NAME_____ FIRST_____ MIDDLE_____ PHONE_____ SEX_____ STUDENT NO._____

ADDRESS_____ SOPHOMORE (3 credits)_____ JUNIOR (8 credits)_____ SENIOR (12 credits)_____

DATE_____

REGISTRATION PROCEDURES

1. Using ink, fill in your name, address, phone, sex, grade classification, and student number on the registration card. Do NOT write anything anything else on the card; your teachers will fill in the class schedule as you enroll in their classes. Be sure that you have filled out the rest of your registration materials.

2. Be sure that you have completed a tentative class schedule on Part A of the "Student's Copy of Program" form. You may use any of the course titles listed on the master schedule for which you meet the prerequisites in making up your tentative class schedule.

3. Check Part A of the "Student's Copy of Program" against the "Closed Classes" listed on the chalkboards to ensure that the classes you want have not been closed. If a class you wanted has been closed, re-work your tentative schedule or move one of your alternate selections into the closed class spot.

4. If you cannot reconcile a conflict in your program, get assistance from a Counselor or Student Helper.

5. When you are ready to enroll, report to each one of your scheduled teachers. As you enroll be sure you receive an IBM class card from each teacher.

6. Be sure your student number has been filled in on each of your IBM cards.

7. After you have finished, fill out Part B of the "Student's Copy of Program", prior to "checking out" of the registration area.

8. Report to the "Check-out Station". Turn in the yellow registration card, IBM cards, and any other requested forms; keep the "Student's Copy of Program" so that you will have a schedule of your classes, room numbers, and teachers to use on the first day that classes meet.

9. Students who do not register on their appointed day may be counted truant unless the student's parent calls in for an excused absence.

10. If you miss your appointment time you may come in any time during registration after your appointment time.

SEMESTER	COURSE TITLES	PHASES	ROOM NUMBERS	TEACHER'S NUMBERS	TEACHER'S INITIALS
1.					
2.					
3.					
4.					
5.					
6.					
7.					

SOPHOMORES ONLY: YOU MUST ENROLL IN THE FOLLOWING TWO CLASSES

1. _____
2. _____

FIGURE 6.8. Keysort Registration Card. (Western High School.)

has provided a detailed description of the nongraded high school program and registration pattern.[3]

Another variation for registering students is required for the *Indi Flex S* Model of scheduling described by Manlove and Beggs.[4] GASP, the story of school scheduling by computers, involves registration patterns similar to those used in SSSS scheduling described earlier in this chapter.[5]

RESOLVING SCHEDULING
CONFLICTS BY MACHINES

Various mechanical and electronic devices have been constructed to speed up the process of resolving conflicts. Surprisingly, the technique utilized by machines is similar to that used with the conventional conflict or matrix sheet discussed in Chapter Three. The most widely used machine systems are the *marginal key-sort device* which is operated manually in part; and *computerized* or *electronic data processing,* which can be programmed for various purposes. Both systems are being utilized more extensively in schools.

The Marginal Key-Sort Punch Card. The marginal key-punch or key-sort device serves the same purpose as the conflict sheet in locating scheduling conflicts. In using the key-sort system, the margins of student registration cards are notched by subjects and then sorted. (A marginal key-punch card is illustrated in Figure 16, Chapter Two.) To check conflicts for single section courses, all cards for a certain grade are placed in a box or bin, and a sorting tool is inserted in the marginal holes to isolate a specific course, such as biology. The cards notched for other courses remain in the box. To check for conflicts between biology and French II on the sorted biology cards, the tool is in-

---

[3]B. Frank Brown, *The Nongraded High School,* (Englewood Cliffs, N.J.: Prentice Hall, Inc., 1963), pp. 136-141.

[4]Donald C. Manlove and David W. Beggs, III, *Flexible Scheduling,* (Bloomington: Indiana University Press, 1966).

[5]Judith Murphy and Robert Sutter, *School Scheduling by Computer—The Story of GASP* (New York: Educational Facilities Laboratories, 1964).

serted in the holes punched for French II, allowing those cards *without* biology and French conflicts to remain in the box. This information is then recorded on a conflict sheet. The process is continued with each single section cluster of cards until all conflicts have been recorded. Resolution of conflicts is considerably eased when students are required to list alternate courses during preregistration or registration.

Matulis has recommended the use of marginal punch in his explanation of the total scheduling process, with the result that a school of 1500 students using this system can increase the speed of registration so that full operation can be reached on the second day of school with a minimum of errors or changes.[6]

Electronic Data Processing. In electronic data processing, each student inserts data on mark-sense cards by designating code numbers for the courses to be taken with a special electrographic pencil. This data is compiled, punched, and transferred to appropriate cards from which an "audit" schedule is programmed to reject those cards with conflicts. The counselor or individual responsible for this operation then repunches rejected cards using alternate course requests and feeds them back into the machine. When all conflicts have been resolved in this manner, a Master Schedule is made on a print-out.

Once the "bugs" in computer programming are eliminated, such techniques do speed up the technical processes of registration and schedule building. In the beginning, human error caused by inexperience may create problems, but, once problems are corrected, detailed work related to scheduling can be concluded rapidly.

The current operative and rental costs of computer hardware and software may be beyond the budgetary capabilities of individual districts. In some instances, several districts have pooled their finances to install a data processing center, as was done, for example in the intermediate school district of Oakland County Schools of Pontiac, Michigan. In other cases, electronic data processing services may be purchased from a commercial agency or a university. The use of commercial services deserves

---

[6]Anthony S. Matulis, "Foolproof Scheduling in Record Time," *School Management* 5 (March 1960): 69-74.

careful study, for many are neither programmed nor oriented toward school schedules, but, rather are geared toward business and industrial problems. A complete understanding of the types of data needed for computerized scheduling is of vital importance. In all probability, the participating school or schools should have a specialist on the staff to be certain that information is programmed as needed. Otherwise, unrelated information and numerous delays can result.

Constructing the Schedule by Computer. Several of the steps discussed in the construction of a conventional schedule can be completed effectively by data processing, if trained personnel are available to coordinate and administer the total process. The details of registration by machine were discussed in Chapter Two. However, since the process of registration is closely related to schedule construction, the preliminary steps will be reviewed to demonstrate the continuity of the total process. Larger high schools using team-teaching and modular time units normally need to use some type of computer scheduling because of the complex processes required by such projects.[7]

The basic steps in computerized scheduling are outlined below.

1. The registration card is punched and printed. It contains the student's name, grade, sex, and other related basic information.
2. Students preregister by inserting data in code number form for selected classes on a special card sometimes with a special pencil.
3. The initial data cards are punched, sorted by classes, and a computer *print-out* of the number of students requesting each class is obtained.
4. This print-out is forwarded to the faculty by departments or teams, and they, in turn, check the number of sections needed, determine staffing needs by the number of sections to be taught, and forward this information to the personnel office.

---

[7]Robert N. Bush, "Decision for the Principal; Hand or Computer Scheduling," *Bulletin of the N.A.S.S.P.* (April 1964): 141-46.

5. The department chairmen receive a print-out verifying the number of teachers available, the number of students, and the number of classes to be offered based on philosophical and fiscal policies.

6. The faculty in each department develops a *structure* utilizing accreditation standards, state department time requirements, and other factors previously discussed. If the schedule is conventional, structuring is relatively simple, but if a form of modular scheduling and team-teaching is used, rather complex decisions on how these modules will be utilized in weekly, biweekly, or monthly cycles and how the number of phases (large group, small group, and laboratory) will be assigned their proportional time units must be made.

7. This information is tabulated on a *consolidation sheet* and forwarded to the individual in the school responsible for the scheduling program. An illustration of such a consolidation sheet is provided in Figure 6.9.

Teacher *Courses*		*Totals*

Department _____

D.C. _____ (Initial)

FIGURE 6.9. Portion of a Consolidation Sheet. (Reprinted by courtesy of Valley High School, Clark County School District, Las Vegas, Nevada.)

Data from the *consolidation sheet* is transferred to a *master structure sheet* which then provides the basic scheduling information to be forwarded to the computer. All late enrollments are hand or machine punched and included with this master structure sheet.

8. An *audit schedule* is then run and the conflicts and inconsistencies located. A tentative master schedule is also printed out to be used as a guide in resolving the conflicts. The conflicts are resolved, repunched, and returned to the computer.

9. The *final translate* from the computer generally includes the following: student schedules, a master schedule, a teacher schedule, a room schedule, and a class list for each section and phase, if this type of program is utilized. Schedules by cycles are also available if team-teaching and modular scheduling are practiced.

Constructing the School Schedule Using the Marginal or Key Punch Card System.   The steps in schedule construction using the marginal or key punch card are quite similar to those in computer scheduling. However, a different device is employed in the actual implementation of some phases of the procedure.

1. Registration is completed on the marginal or key punch card (see Figure 6.10 for a sample of this type of card). These cards are often color coded to represent the different grade levels.

2. Cards are punched or notched around the margin for each course in which the student is registered.

3. The cards are then placed in a bin and a long key or rod is inserted into a specified numbered hole, the key is lifted, and the registrations for that course are tallied.

4. The cards are sorted again to determine conflicts between the single section cards (see Chapter Two).

5. The Master Schedule is then constructed by using a mosaic type board, adding room assignments, and other specific information.

6. Copies of the card are distributed to both advisory or homeroom teachers and the students.

FIGURE 6.10. Marginal or Key-sort Punch Card. (Courtesy, Western High School, Clark County School District, Las Vegas, Nevada.)

PRE-REGISTRATION CARD

(please do not fold or mutilate)

NAME WACHTER KATHY S.
(last) (first) (initial)

Sophomore (3credits) ✓ Junior (6credits) ___ Senior (12credits) ___

DATE OF BIRTH 8 8 1951
(month) (day) (year)

SEX: Male ___ Female ✓

FALL SEMESTER (Course Titles)	PHASE
1.	
2.	
3.	
4.	
5. * Enrichment Course (if desired)	

ALTERNATE COURSE CHOICES
1.
2.
3.

Kathy Wachter
(Student's Signature)

Failure to return this Registration Card with parent's signature will result in a delay in registration which may cause a student to forfeit his first choice of subject or teacher.

* Students wishing to enroll in a sixth class may do so during the Enrichment Period which meets one hour prior to the beginning of the regular school day. School district busses will be scheduled to arrive at the beginning of the regular school day.

SPRING SEMESTER (Course Titles)	PHASE	
1. INTERMEDIATE FRENCH	4	½
2. BIOLOGY II	3	½
3. RECENT U.S. HISTORY	4-5	½
4. GENERAL BUSINESS	3	½
5. ORIENTATION	1	½
CO-EDUCATIONAL P.E.	3-4	¼
* Enrichment Course (if desired)		

ALTERNATE COURSE CHOICES
1.
2.
3.

Mrs. Henry E. Wachter
(Parent's Signature)

It is understood that students may need of or want to change to subjects listed as Alternates without getting an additional authorization from the parent.

Machine printing devices are now available which can translate the punched information to a print-out sheet. This class list can then be made available to faculty members upon very short notice. Some schools utilizing daily demand schedules employ this type of device to print out daily schedules from the marginal key punch card. Regardless of the system used, students should receive a copy of these schedules and a necessary guide to class attendance.

VARIABLE OR FLEXIBLE SCHEDULING

The emphasis now shifts from the use of mechanical and electronic devices in scheduling to newer approaches to instructional programming. One of the major problems related to conventional scheduling is the fixed and rigid time restriction placed upon the teacher by the uniform class period. All lessons, assignments, and projects are indirectly controlled by the forty, fifty, or sixty minute time frame. For example, if a teacher has a fifty minute film and the class has a duration of only forty-five minutes, what does he do? How can he plan on a special project or discussion when the period assigned does not permit time for the needed learning experience of the student?

As a result of this situation, there have been various attempts to alter or vary the time period to give the flexibility needed in the teaching-learning process. In short, the time factor alone should not be considered the basic determinate of teaching strategies. Numerous plans have been devised to modify the fixed and conventional class time period concept. Some are quite basic in nature, while others have evolved as highly complex patterns of operation requiring considerable planning for computerized schedule development. A number of these techniques developed to provide for flexible instructional programming will be reviewed in the following paragraphs.

Double Periods. One of the earliest attempts to adapt the class-time frame to a specific instructional need was the introduction of the double-period class. Originally, this innovation was conceived in order to provide more time for laboratory courses and is still used widely for this purpose in secondary schools today. The problem with this technique arises in scheduling the student during the double-period "off" days. In other words, how is the student to use the time on days when double periods are not needed? Generally, these students are either assigned to study halls or to health and physical education classes on days when lab activities do not occupy the second period of the double-period combination. A typical double period schedule might follow the pattern shown in Figure 6.11.

Period	Monday	Tuesday	Wednesday	Thursday	Friday
1	Chem. I	Chem. I Lab	Chem. I	Chem. I Lab	Chem. I
2	Study Hall or P.E.	Chem. I Lab	Study Hall or P.E.	Chem. I Lab	Study Hall or P.E.
3	Biology	Biol. Lab	Biology	Biol. Lab	Biology
4	Health or Study Hall	Biol. Lab	Health or Study Hall	Biol. Lab	Health or Study Hall

FIGURE 6.11. Double Period Schedule.

As more elective courses have become available to the student and as sizes of school enrollments have increased, the number of conflicts through the use of double periods has also increased. The double period has become a constant source of frustration, for it has been difficult to resolve the conflicts it has generated within the conventional schedule.

Back-to-Back Scheduling. The junior-high program normally has a block-of-time schedule for its required courses, many of which are grouped into core areas. If the core courses are scheduled back-to-back, the teacher or teachers have the flexibility of two periods for both core subjects. For example, a portion of the schedule might be designed for the core subjects only in the manner shown in Figure 6.12.

Note that in the preceding example the group of students meets in the same room and possibly with the same teacher for

	Period	Daily	
Total of 90 min.	1 (45 min.)	Room 23 Lang. Arts 7 Miss X	Group A
	2 (45 min.)	Room 23 Soc. Sc. 7 Miss X	Group A
	3	Regular Class Period	

FIGURE 6.12. Example of Back-to-Back Scheduling.

more than one period. The result of placing these students and subjects back-to-back is to provide a greater time variance (ninety minutes as opposed to forty-five for each class) for implementing teaching plans. In this situation, two teachers could easily work together to organize a time utilization chart that would accommodate for unexpected changes even at the last moment. Typically, periods of forty-five minutes duration are preferred by teachers for double periods.

For many years, the traditional time span for a class period has resulted in a restrictive time cell which automatically constrained innovative team-teaching projects. A school contemplating the installation of teacher teams in a limited number of subjects would face the time restriction of the conventional class period almost immediately. A solution to this dilemma is illustrated in the following paragraphs.

For example, assume that it was decided in School A to do some team-teaching in biology, a course required of all sophomores, a total of eighty students. The class period of fifty minutes did not allow the time flexibility demanded for the large-group, small-group, and independent study patterns of team teaching. To provide additional time, the English Department decided to set up teams to teach English 2, a course also required of all sophomores and involving the same eighty students. If these two large groups were scheduled back-to-back with the two teaching teams in English 2 and biology, the combined time unit would total 100 minutes (or more if the time between periods were added). The back-to-back schedule would then be divided into modular units with the English and biology teams meeting regularly to construct a time-use chart for both subjects. Since only two subjects are involved, a great amount of programming flexibility would be available to each team.*

Period	Daily*
	Rooms 204, 206, and 208
1	Biology 2
50 min.	Team 80 Students
2	English 2
50 min.	Team 80 Students
3	Regular Classes
50 min.	(Students go to various courses in schedule)

*Schedule varies daily with team planning. Biology, for example, may not meet at all on some days, depending upon the instructional plan.

FIGURE   6.13. Back-to-Back   Schedule   for   Team Teaching.

The size of the school enrollment is not a major factor in determining the type of instructional programming. Since only the two or three courses directly involved need to be organized, the number of students may be limited within these classes. For example, a team back-to-back schedule may be desired for the top ability groups only. The other students in the same subjects would continue to attend the conventional time schedules during the day. The teacher would be a team member only during that one unit of time and then return to a conventional schedule for the remainder of the day.

				Periods					
Teacher	Homeroom 8:45-3:57	I 9:00-9:57	II 10:00-10:57	III 11:00-11:57	Lunch 12:00-12:40	IV 12:40-1:37	V 1:40-2:37	VI 2:40-3:37
Miss A	8th 219	Eighth, English, Social Studies	Eighth, English, Social Studies	Conference		Eighth, English, Social Studies		Conference
Mr. B	8th 320	Eighth, English, Social Studies	Eighth, English, Social Studies	Eighth Reading		Ungraded 8-9 Eng.	Remedial 8th Eng.	Conference
Mrs. C	7th 217	Remedial 8th Eng.	Ungraded 10-11 Eng.	Ungraded 8-9 Eng.		Seventh Reading	Confer-ence	Reading Testing
Mrs. D	7th 114	Eighth, English, Social Studies	Eighth, English, Social Studies	Conference		Seventh Reading	Eighth, English, Social Studies	
Miss E	7th 216	Confer-ence	Seventh, English, Social Studies ⟶				Seventh, English, Social Studies	

FIGURE 6.14. Portion of a Block-Time Schedule.[8]

[8]Lester W. Anderson and Lauren A. Van Dyke, *Secondary School Administration*, (Boston: Houghton Mifflin Company, 1963), p. 162. Reprinted by permission of the publisher.

143

Auto Mechanics II and III		Block	Mr. J. Waldron Phase 3-5 Room 850	Block	
Auto Service Techniques (Voc.)	Block	Mr. J. Waldron Phase 3-4 Room 850	Block		
Woodworking I				Mr. D. Vickmark Phase 1-5 Room 820	
Woodworking II			Mr. D. Vickmark Phase 3-5 Room 820		
Electronics I (Voc.)	Block	Mr. J. Casino Phase 3-4 Room 840	Block	Block	Mr. J. Casino Phase 3-4 Room 840	Block

FIGURE 6.15. Portion of a Senior High School Schedule on Block-Time Plan. (Courtesy, Western High School, Clark County School District, Las Vegas, Nevada.)

Block-Time Scheduling. As variation of the back-to-back and double-period plans, the block-time schedule has proved to be an interesting mutation in programs requiring a special type of flexibility. Junior high schools and middle schools utilizing a combination of core subjects, with teaching teams in some subjects and nongrading in other areas, have found the block-time plan most useful. Senior high schools emphasizing certain special programs for students have been able to coordinate their block-time and conventional patterns with little difficulty.

Anderson and Van Dyke have described a junior-high block-time schedule adapted from a Webster Groves, Missouri, secondary school. Figure 6.16 depicts a portion of this model. A block-time schedule at the senior high school level is illustrated in Figure 6.14.

Extended Period-Floating Schedule. In an effort to provide more time for teacher-planning, supervised study, and instructional flexibility, several secondary schools have adopted an extended-period plan. These periods are usually of a duration of seventy minutes and meet four times per week, with the fifth period revolved or floated in the schedule to facilitate flexibility. Anderson has reported on this particular scheduling practice in Michigan and listed the following advantages of the extended period-revolving schedule plan.

1. More time for supervised study
2. Elimination of large, often ineffective study halls
3. Time provided for laboratory classes and field trips
4. Provision for longer activity periods if scheduled in the daily schedule[9]

A sample floating schedule is illustrated in Figure 6.16; English 2 is the floating subject.

This type of schedule could remain the same throughout the semester, or a different revolving pattern could be designed at certain intervals. Cycles or changes sometimes have to be established as often as every two weeks, although a six-week or nine-

---

[9]Lester W. Anderson, "What is the Most Effective Way of Arranging the Length and Use of the Class Period?" *The Bulletin of the NASSP* (April, 1959): 162.

Period	Monday	Tuesday	Wednesday	Thursday	Friday
1	W. Hist.	W. Hist.	W. Hist.	W. Hist.	Eng. 2
2	Math	Math	Math	Eng. 2	Math
3	Biol.	Biol.	Advisory Homeroom Activity	Biol.	Biol.
4	Span. I	Eng. 2	Span. I	Span. I	Span. I
5	Eng. 2	P.E.	P.E.	P.E.	P.E.

FIGURE 6.16. Floating Schedule with English 2 the Floating Subject.

week quarter system appears to be more practical. The longer periods do provide time for the teachers to work on an individual basis to a greater extent than in the conventional time unit of fifty to fifty-five minutes. The flexibility is derived from within the larger time cell itself and not so much from the arrangement of the periods.

Varied-Period Scheduling. Anderson and Van Dyke have reported on the varied-period scheduling practices some secondary schools have attempted in their effort to break away from the conventional pattern of scheduling. Actually, the varied-period schedule is an adaptation of the scheduling pattern used by colleges and universities and requires that the secondary school move to a semester schedule. Generally, multiples of the Carnegie unit are employed and interpreted by using the college system of credit hours. A sample varied-period schedule program for an eleventh grade student is depicted in Figure 6.17. Note that some courses meet only two or three times per week, while others meet six or seven periods per week. Each course carries five semester hours of credit.

MODULAR OR FLEXIBLE SCHEDULING

In May of 1956, the Executive Committee of the National Association of Secondary School Principals appointed a Commission

Period	Monday	Tuesday	Wednesday	Thursday	Friday
I 8:15	American Literature Lecture	Quiz-Study Section B	American Literature Lecture	Quiz-Study Section B	American Literature Lecture
II 9:15	French III	Art III	French III	Art III	French III
III 10:15	American History Lecture	American History Lecture	American History Lecture	Quiz-Study Section D	Quiz-Study Section D
IV 11:15	Algebra IV		Algebra IV		Algebra IV
V 1:00	Physical Education		Physical Education		Physical Education
VI 2:00	Chemistry	Chemistry	Chemistry	Chemistry	Chemistry
VII 3:00	Band	Laboratory	Band	Laboratory	Band

FIGURE 6.17. A Varied-Schedule Program for an Eleventh Grade Student.[10]

Period	Monday	Tuesday	Wednesday	Thursday	Friday	Saturday
8:30 9:00	Large Group Instruction	Individual Study	Large Group	Large Group	Large Group	
9:30 10:00 10:30 11:00	Small Group Discussion		Small Group		Small Group	Individual
					Individual Study	
11:30	Large Group Instruction	Large Group Instruction	Large Group	Individual		
12:00	Lunch and Activities					
1:00 1:30	Individual Study	Small Group	Small Group	Small Group	Large Group	
2:00 2:30		Large Group	Individual Study			Individual
3:00 3:30		Individual Study		Individual Study	Small Group	
	Small Group					

FIGURE 6.18. How a Student Might Spend Time in the Secondary School of the Future.[11]

[10]Anderson and Van Dyke, *Secondary School Administration,* p. 164.

[11]J. Lloyd Trump, *Images of the Future* (Urbana, Illinois: Commission on the Experimental Study of the Utilization of Staff in the Secondary School, 1959), p. 12. Reprinted by permission of the author.

on the Experimental Study of Utilization of Staff in the Secondary School. The outgrowth of this commission report by J. Lloyd Trump in 1959 resulted in a proposal for "team-teaching" and subsequent *modular* or *flexible* scheduling related to this reorganization of instruction. Trump outlined how a student might spend time in the secondary school of the future. Figure 6.18 diagrams this schedule.

The Modular Unit. The module generally is defined as a unit of time ten to thirty minutes in length, with periods of from twelve to fifteen minutes most commonly used as modules. A unit is often defined by the number of pupils involved in that particular subject. The modular unit, therefore, identifies the number of students, amount of time they might have, the size of the group, and the subject. For example:

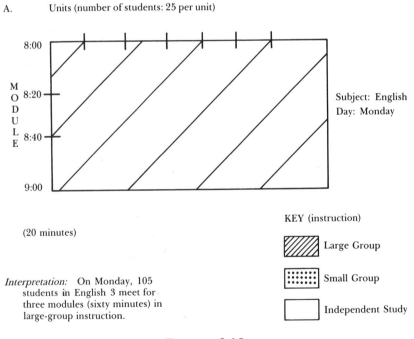

A.   Units (number of students: 25 per unit)

Subject: English
Day: Monday

(20 minutes)

KEY (instruction)

Large Group

Small Group

Independent Study

Interpretation: On Monday, 105 students in English 3 meet for three modules (sixty minutes) in large-group instruction.

FIGURE 6.19

If ability grouping, or phasing, is also involved and the entire school operates on a team-teaching organizational plan, the

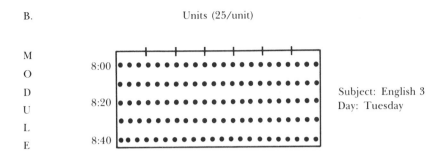

Interpretation: On Tuesday, seven sections of students,
fifteen per section, meet for small-group instruction.

FIGURE 6.20

complexity of the schedule immediately becomes evident. Hand
scheduling is, for all practical purposes, an impossible task to
perform in this situation. Thus, some adaptation of computer
scheduling is required. Various computer techniques have been
developed and are currently being employed by schools across
the country. Some of the more noted organizations able to develop Master Schedules in working with flexible scheduling in
team teaching programs are included in the following list.

1. *Stanford School Scheduling System* (SSSS). This computer scheduling system at Stanford University was one of
   the first programmed to develop Master Schedules on the
   team-teaching, flexible (modular) scheduling concept.
   The project was originally established under a grant from
   the Fund for the Advancement of Education and is administered by the Stanford University School of Education.
2. *Generalized Academic Simulation Programs* (GASP).[12]
   Developed in 1963–64 at about the same time as the Stanford Project, GASP was initiated not only to program
   student sectioning, but also to develop the Master Schedule for experimental schools. Affiliated with the Educa-

---

[12]Judith Murphy and Robert Sutter, *School Scheduling by Computer - The Story of
GASP* (New York: Educational Facilities Laboratories, 1964).

tional Facilities Laboratories in New York and funded by
the Ford Foundation, GASP has become directly involved
in computer scheduling for interested schools across the
nation.

3. *IBM 7070 or 7040 CLASS* (Class Load and Student
Scheduling). The services of this organization are used by
numerous schools across the nation. The outputs are student conflicts, the master schedule print-out, and individual student schedule print outs.

4. The *Indi Flex S Model.* The title refers primarily to a
model and the development of guidelines for planning a
flexible schedule rather than to a specific computer unit.
Manlove and Beggs have outlined the rationale, use of
special facilities, and the actual schedule preparation procedures for flexible scheduling. Their report was based on
a survey of thirty-three schools using some form of flexible scheduling. Utilizing this information, they have developed the Indiana Flexible Schedule (Indi-Flex-S)
which can be adapted according to the professional judg-
ment of the principals concerned.[13]

5. *Other agencies* investigating the development of school
Master Schedules are Systems Development Corporation
in Santa Monica, California; the National Cash Register
Corporation; and the California State Department of Edu-
cation's new Center for Research and Development in
Educational Data Processing at Sacramento.

Daily Demand Scheduling. One of the more unique flexible
scheduling programs recently developed is the Daily Demand
Schedule. Constructed on the premise that a schedule is not
totally flexible unless it correlates the efforts of administrators,
teachers and students, the Daily Demand Schedule directly involves all of those individuals in the scheduling process on a
day-to-day basis. The general pattern is for departments or
teams to work out a weekly schedule of basic required courses
and then, using these as a foundation, have the students individ-

---

[13]Donald C. Manlove and David W. Beggs, III, *Flexible Scheduling* (Bloomington:
Indiana University Press, 1966).

ually schedule their classes daily during a ten or twelve minute period each morning.

Brookhurst Junior High School in the Anaheim, California, Union High School District employs a Daily Demand Schedule for its more than 800 eighth and ninth graders. The 400 seventh graders are scheduled on a block-time basis because of their core program. Brookhurst inaugurated the Daily Demand Schedule in 1962 through the combined efforts of the community, parents, staff, and administrators using these basic assumptions as guidelines:

1. All subjects do not require the same amount of time or method of instruction.
2. All students do not have equal abilities nor do they learn at the same rate.
3. The teacher is best quaiified to determine the student's academic needs, the method of instruction, and the time required.[14]

The following is an explanation of the *Daily Demand Schedule* as utilized by the Brookhurst Junior High School in Anaheim, California.

Modules. The school day has been divided into sixteen modules of twenty minutes each. Each disciplinary team may group its students as it desires; i.e., English may have three or four ability groups, history only one. Students within these groups may be changed at the teacher's request, and new groups may be formed without disrupting a schedule.

Lesson Job Order. Each teaching team submits five daily lesson job orders to the scheduling office on Monday for one week hence. On the daily form they indicate in Column I the total number of students in each group. For example: Pre-Algebra may consist of 200 students, so this number would be indicated. In the next column is requested the number of modules desired. The team may indicate one module for a large-group lecture or fourteen for a field trip. A third column indicates the number of students wanted in each class; e.g., the ten or 200 mentioned

[14]"The Daily Demand Schedule." A brochure describing the program at Brookhurst Junior High School, Anaheim Union High School District, Anaheim, California. Reprinted by permission of Don Nielsen, Principal, Brookhurst Junior High School.

before. Specific modules may be requested in the next column, but this is usually left to the discretion of the scheduling office unless a guest speaker is requested. Should additional instructional help be requested, teachers are asked to indicate the type of instruction planned to facilitate assigning rooms; e.g., large-group instruction, small-group discussion, etc. This information may also be used as a record by which the team may evaluate units at their completion. [*See Figure 6.21 for an example of the form used by each team or department.*]

The job orders are then sorted by the office into three categories:

1. *Office Schedule.*   Classes scheduled from job orders of this category provide the student no choice in the selection of subject or time. The subject, room number, and modules will be printed on the schedule before he receives it. All office-scheduled subjects are then transposed onto the teacher's schedule, and each teacher given a copy which verifies where he is to be and at what time. Across the top, the subject is indicated; the left hand column shows the modules the class will meet, the numbers under the subject heading are rooms and the circles indicate the inclusive time for each class. Special bulletin notices are also placed on the teacher's schedule.

2. *Must Schedule.*   Classes scheduled from job orders of this category provide for the teacher to control the subject, but the student may select the time he wishes to attend the class. Physical education serves as a good example. The student must attend each day according to a state law, but the teachers are not concerned with what time of the day he attends class.

3. *May Schedule.*   Classes scheduled from job orders of this category allow the student to control both the time and the subject. These classes are generally from his elective program, but are not necessarily so. Any teacher may put his classes on the May Schedule, and this is often done for students needing make-up or remedial work in the academic areas. These are scheduled in addition to, not in lieu of, the regular academic commitment.

Electives.   Most of the electives operate on a contract or agreement basis. During the summer a course description of the electives offered is mailed home for the parents and students to use in selecting electives for the coming semester. Elective teachers are encouraged to work out curricular courses of study in which the student may spend varying amounts of time from day to day and from week to week.

From _____ Teacher — Subject

Date Needed _____

Name of Group	Total Number in Group	Number of Modules	Number of Groups	Number of Teachers Per Group	Class Size Request	Module Request	Room Request	Type of Scheduling	Method of Instruction (Large or small group, Ind. Study)

Bulletin: _____

Attention: _____

Approved: _____
Team Leader

FIGURE 6.21. Lesson Job Order by Department: Daily Demand Schedule. (Brookside Junior High School, Anaheim, California.)

Units of credit from one to ten may be earned as the student finds time to work with the elective. The amount of credit depends upon the number of projects that the student has completed at the end of the grading period. Teachers are encouraged to individualize the types of projects and the number required for a particular grade if at all possible.

Students may change their elective program as the year progresses, providing the grade-level counselor and parents agree to the alteration. Students are encouraged, however, to complete at least a minimal number of projects before dropping a course. There is no limit to the number of subjects a student may take. An extremely qualified student may take as many as ten electives during the course of a year.

Teachers add new subjects as the need arises and disband classes when their usefulness is fulfilled. The program coordinator is, of course, involved in all decisions affecting their daily schedule.

The "must" and "may" schedule categories are transposed onto a Daily Master Schedule which is distributed to the student each morning by his counseling teacher along with his individual program. The counseling group composed of twenty to twenty-five students meets from 8:10 to 8:30 each morning, and it is during this time that the student fills in his remaining open modules as he can accommodate them. The counseling teacher then checks to see that all "must" classes are met, that all 16 modules have been filled, that the student has elected a program which will be in his best interests (well-balanced and suited to his needs), and that any information pertinent to this individual is passed on to him; e.g., special music or athletic instructions. (*Figure 6.22 illustrates one day's Master Schedule and student work sheet.*)

The counseling teacher separates the schedules before returning the top copy to the student for him to follow that day. The last copy is alphabetized and filed in the office so that a student may be found at any time.

Attendance. Attendance is taken in the "Office Schedule" classes from a print-out list made in the office. Must and May schedule attendance is by a spot-check process in the classes at regular intervals. Any suspected problem attendance students are checked regularly by the attendance counselor, and there is continual hall checking for attendance irregularities.

Rm.
No.   *Subjects Offered*

Library Is Closed Mods 2-4 Today.

Art· (8 Art: 2 consecutive mods only)

26   8 Art: 2-3, 4-5, 8-9, 11-12, 13-14, 15-16 (Must)
25   9 App Art: 6-7 (Must)
*25   9 Art: 2-5, 8, 10-13 (May)

Business

Off   Nurse OP: 6-7, 8-9, 11-12, 15-16 (Must)
 14   Gen Bus: 2-3, 4-5 (May)
 14   Gen Bus Lab: 8-9 (May)
*31   Type: 2-9, 11-16 (May)
Lib   Lib Prac: 2-3, 4-5, 6-7, 8, 9, 10, 11-12, 13-14, 15-16 (Off)

English (9 Eng: If you have a conflict, sched any class. Miss Miller's Grp II:
      sched any 2 mods)

      8 Eng IA & IB: may sched with Grp II.
  5   8 Eng Gr II A-K: 2-3, 6-7, 8-9, 11-12, 13-14, 15-16 (Must)
  2   8 Eng II L-Z: 2-3, 4-5, 6-7, 8-9, 13-14, 15-16 (Must)
  3   9 Eng I: 6-7, 13-14, 15-16 (Must)
  4   9 Eng I: 2-3, 13-14 (Must)
  3   9 Eng II: 2-3, 4-5, 11-12 (Must)
* 4   9 Eng II: 4-8, 10 (Must)
*23   Read: 13-16 (May)
  1   Drama: 2-3, 6-7 (May [Pantomimes] (2 mods)
  1   Speech: 4-5 (May) [Impromptu]
      Drama & Speech Sched only 1 class per day

Home Ec   (Home Furnish: May 14 mod 11-12 — Hester-Mills)

39   H Ec: 2-3, 4-5, 6-7, 8-9, 13-14, 15-16 (Must)

Foreign Languages

*16   Fren A: 6, 7, 9 / Fren B: 11, 12, 14 (Must)
*13   Span A: 3, 4, 5, 13, 14, 16 (Must)
 14   Span B Hawk: 13-14 (Must)
 12   Span I: 13-14 (Must)
*16   All Fren: 6, 7, 11, 12, 14 (May)
*13   Span Lab: 7, 12 (May)

155

*16 Fren A-I: 9/ Fren B: 8/ Fren II: 13 (Off)
*13 Span B: 2, 6, 11, 15 (Off)

Industrial Arts (2 mods only please)

* 9 Draft: 2-7, 9, 10 (May)
*10 Metal: 9-14 (May)
*11 Wood: 2-7, 13, 14 (May)
  9 Draft: 2-3, 6-7, 9-10, 13-14, 15-16 (Off)
 10 Metal: 2-3, 4-5, 6-7, 9-10, 11-12, 13-14 (Off)

Math

 8 9 Alg: 2-3, 8-9, 11-12, 15-16 (Must)
 6 8&9 Pre Alg: 15-16 (Must)
 7 8&9 Pre Alg: 2-3 (Must)
 8 8&9 Pre Alg: 4-5, 6-7, 13-14 (Must)
 6 8&9 Gen Math: 2-3, 6-7, 13-14 (Must)
 7 8&9 Gen Math: 11-12 (Must)
 7 8 K II: 4-5, 6-7, 8-9, 13-14, 15-16 (Must)
 6 8&9 Lay Math [Flex] : 4 (Must)
 6 8&9 Lay Math [Rigid] : 11-12 (Must)
* 6 8&9 MM 2: 5, 10 (Must)
 6 Labs: 8, 9 (May)
 4 Labs: 11 (May)

Music

 38 Adv Band: 2-3 (Must)
 37 CC: 4-5 / Adv & Int G: 11-12 (Must)
 37 Sm Grp: 2-3/ Boys: 8-9 Beg G: 13-14, 15-16 (May)
*38 Prac Rms: 2-9, 11-14 (May)
 37 Int B   BB Brass   BB Woods   Beg O
    8-9   11-12   13-14   15-16 (May)
 38 Adv O: 6-7 (Off)

Phys Ed (BPE: 2 mods only please)

 G Adapt BPE: 2-3, 4-5 (Must)
   Adapt GPE: 13-14, 15-16 (Must)
 G BPE: Open 2-3/ V Ball: 4-5, 11-12
   SB: 6-7/ Tramp: 8-9/ 8 F B: 13-14
   Wrestling & 9 BB: 15-16 (Must)
 G GPE: Softball: 2-3, 6-7, 13-14, 15-16
   Tennis: 4-5, 6-7, 8-9, 11-12, 15-16
   Self Defense: 13-14 (Must)
 G COED Softball: 4-5, 8-9, 11-12 (Must)
 G Spec BPE: 2-3 (Off)

Science

```
*24   9 Sci I: 2-6 (Must)
 24   9 Gen Sci: 11-12, 13-14, 15-16 (Must)
 18   8 Sci: Copepods: 4-5 (Must)
*18   8 Sci: P1 P2 P3 P4 P5 P6
              11 12 13 14 15 3   (Must)
 17   8 Sci L10-12: 11-12, 13-14, 15-16 (Must)
 17   8 Sci: L-6  L-7  L-8  L-9
             2-3  4-5   6-7  8-9  (Must)
*18   8 Sci P1-5: 6, 7, 8, 16 (May)
*24   9 Sci I: 7 (Off)
```

Social Science

```
*33   G Dec: GR A: 6/ Gr B: 7 (Must)
*32   9 Hist Lab: 5-7, 11-14 (May)
*33   8 Hist (All): 2-4, 13-16 (May)
*34   8 Hist (All): 2-4, 13-16 (May)
Lib   8 Hist 'A': 2-4 (Off)
*19   8 Hist (All): 5, 6, 7 (Off)
*20   9 Hist Lecture: 2, 3, 4 (Off)
 32   9 Rigid Hist: 9-10 (Off)

 28   HIP Eng A: 4-5/ Eng B+C: 2-3 (Must)
 28   HIP Read A: 6-7/ Read B+C: 9-10 (Must)
 29   HIP Math A: 13-14/ Math B+C: 11-12 (Must)
 29   HIP Hist A: 9-10 (Must)
 29   HIP Hist B: 4-5 / Hist C: 6-7 (Off)

Lib   Speech Therapy: 2-6, 11, 12, 13, 15 (Off)
Lib   Pre Regis: 2-3, 4-5, 6-7, 11-12, 13-14, 15-16 (Off)

Off   Stu Cab: 2-3 (May)
```

Work Sheet

```
 1._____
 2._____
 3._____
 4._____
 5._____
 6._____
 7._____
 8._____
 9._____
10._____
```

11._____
12._____
13._____
14._____
15._____
16._____

Key

*1 mod classes

FIGURE 6.22. Daily Schedule of Course Offerings.
(Brookside Junior High School, Anaheim, California.)

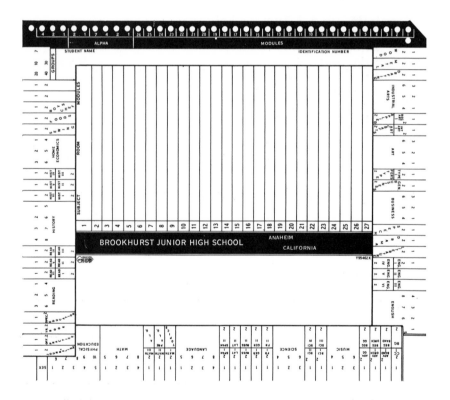

FIGURE 6.23. Daily Key Sort Schedule Card. (Reprinted by Courtesy of Brookhurst Junior High School. Brookhurst recently converted to a computer scheduling process utilizing the same procedures.)

Machine Operations.   Litton Industries, in conjunction with the school staff, has developed a print-out list of office-scheduled classes giving the teacher positive attendance. Also the machines print those office-scheduled classes on the students' schedule card each day. (*Figure 6.22 provides an example of a daily keysort card the student uses in transferring his schedule from the Master Schedule Work Sheet.*) The machines include a photo-reader, a teletype machine, and a small rotary printer.[15]

The time or bell schedule is posted in all rooms and is available to all students. Bells ring only for the seventh graders who use the combination of modules listed on the schedule (Figure 6.24).

Students may enroll into an elective course at any time during the semester. They meet with the instructor, work out goals and projects, and then enroll on a May Schedule whenever they can. Teachers of all elective subjects have "flow charts" outlining the steps students can follow in working out projects toward meeting these goals. They may enroll for from one to ten units of credit and are graded according to achievement upon reaching the goals they have contracted with the teacher. An elective "contract" or "agreement" form is illustrated in Figure 6.25.

A sample *flow chart* for art illustrates how a *contract elective* is organized. (Figure 6.26).

It would appear that schools with smaller enrollments could utilize the daily demand concept and coordinate the process with a limited amount of difficulty. Regardless of size, a school could implement such a program, but this should be done only after careful planning and considerable study. Although time has not permitted research projects to be completed, teachers and students currently involved in this type of scheduling are enthusiastic about their projects.

---

[15]"The Daily Demand Schedule." A brochure describing the program at Brookhurst Junior High School, Anaheim Union High School District, Anaheim, California. Brookhurst recently converted to a computer scheduling process.

Brookhurst Junior High School

7:45	Teacher's Day Begins
8:10	First Bell
8:15 - 8:30	Module 1
8:35 - 8:55	Module 2
9:00 - 9:20	Module 3
9:25 - 9:45	Module 4
9:50 - 10:10	Module 5
10:10 - 10:25	Break
10:25 - 10:45	Module 6
10:50 - 11:10	Module 7
11:15 - 11:35	Module 8
11:40 - 12:00	Module 9
12:05 - 12:25	Module 10
12:30 - 12:50	Module 11
12:55 - 1:15	Module 12
1:20 - 1:40	Module 13
1:45 - 2:05	Module 14
2:10 - 2:30	Module 15
2:35 - 2:55	Module 16
3:25	Teaching Day Ends

FIGURE 6.24. Bell Schedule. (Modules used by Brookhurst Junior High School, Anaheim, California.)

Elective Agreement

Student Name   Subject

Teacher   Date

Counseling Group Teacher   Grade Level

Requirements

1.	_____	6.	_____
2.	_____	7.	_____
3.	_____	8.	_____
4.	_____	9.	_____
5.	_____	10.	_____

Course Grade

Date Completed   Student Signature

FIGURE 6.25. Contract for Elective. (Brookhurst Junior High School, Anaheim, California.)

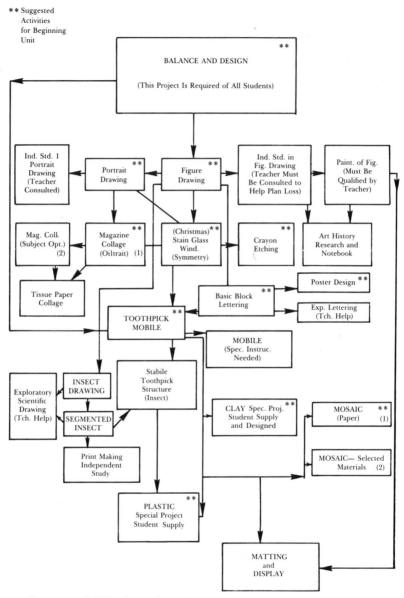

Ninth Grade Art—Projected Course
Contract Elective — Student Selection
Seven Projects Needed to Complete Unit
(Corresponds to One Semester)

**Suggested
Activities
for Beginning
Unit

**
BALANCE AND DESIGN

(This Project Is Required of All Students)

Ind. Std. 1
Portrait
Drawing
(Teacher
Consulted)

Portrait **
Drawing

Figure **
Drawing

Ind. Std. in
Fig. Drawing
(Teacher Must
Be Consulted to
Help Plan Loss)

Paint. of Fig.
(Must Be
Qualified by
Teacher)

Mag. Coll.
(Subject Opt.)
(2)

Magazine **
Collage
(Oiltrait) (1)

(Christmas)**
Stain Glass
Wind.
(Symmetry)

Crayon **
Etching

Art History
Research and
Notebook

Tissue Paper
Collage

Basic Block **
Lettering

Poster Design **

Exp. Lettering
(Tch. Help)

TOOTHPICK **
MOBILE

MOBILE
(Spec. Instruc.
Needed)

INSECT
DRAWING

Stabile
Toothpick
Structure
(Insect)

Exploratory
Scientific
Drawing
(Tch. Help)

SEGMENTED
INSECT

CLAY Spec. Proj. **
Student Supply
and Designed

MOSAIC **
(Paper) (1)

Print Making
Independent
Study

MOSAIC— Selected
Materials (2)

PLASTIC **
Special Project
Student Supply

MATTING
and
DISPLAY

FIGURE 6.26. Sample Flow Chart for Art-Contract
Elective. (Brookhurst Junior High School, Anaheim,
California.)

QUESTIONS AND SUGGESTIONS FOR STUDY

1. How would you go about changing the scheduling processes in your school? Outline the steps you would take.

2. Define flexible scheduling.

3. Can modules be used to replace regular periods in a conventional school program? Explain how this can be done. What would be the value?

4. The variable schedule with a floating period reportedly has some value when a majority of the students are transported. Explain.

5. Conduct a survey of the schools in your area to identify the type of schedules being used. Use the classification listed in this chapter to identify these schedule types.

6. How do the block-time and back-to-back schedules relate to the core curriculum?

7. Construct a *daily demand schedule* in your school. Outline the steps needed to plan this type of schedule.

8. Visit a school which uses a computer to devise its Master Schedule. Note how the conflicts are resolved. How does this differ from the conventional conflict sheet method?

SELECTED REFERENCES

Bossing, Nelson, and Cramer, Roscoe V. *The Junior High School.* Boston: Houghton Mifflin Co., 1965, Chapters 6 and 7, "Block-Time Class Organization" and "The Core Curriculum."

Brown, B. Frank. *The Nongraded High School.* Englewood Cliffs, New Jersey: Prentice-Hall, Inc., 1963, Chapter 6, "Making the Curriculum Meaningful."

Dufay, Frank R. *Ungrading the Elementary School.* West Nyack, New York: Parker Publishing Co., 1966, Chapter 2, "Grouping: The Vital Preliminary."

Jacobson, Paul B.; Reavis, William C.; and Logsdon, James D. *The Effective School Principal,* 2d ed. Englewood Cliffs, New Jersey: Prentice-Hall, Inc., 1963, Chapter 4, "Making a School Schedule."

Linder, Ivan H., and Gunn, Henry M. *Secondary School Administration: Problems and Practices.* Columbus, Ohio: Charles E. Merrill Publishing Co., 1963, Chapter 11, "Schedule Construction and Registration."

Matulis, Anthony S. "Foolproof Scheduling in Record Time." *School Management* 4 (March 1960): 69-74.

Manlove, Donald C., and Beggs, David W. III. *Flexible Scheduling.* Bloomington: Indiana University Press, 1966.

Murphy, Judith, and Sutter, Robert. *School Scheduling by Computer —The Story of GASP.* New York: Educational Laboratory, 1964.

Ovard, Glen F. *Administration of the Changing Secondary School.* New York: The Macmillan Co., 1966, Chapters 6 and 7, "The Annual Cycle—Beginning and Ending the School Year" and "Schedule-Making."

Trump, J. Lloyd. *Images of the Future.* Urbana, Illinois: Commission on the Experimental Study of the Utilization of Staff in the Secondary School, 1959.

Wright, Grace S. "Block-Time Classes and the Core Program in the Junior High School." Bulletin Number 6, U.S. Office of Education. Washington, D.C.: U.S. Government Printing Office, 1950.

Chapter 7

Programming Experiences During the School Year: Trends and Issues in School Calendar Development

An important organizational responsibility of the principal is the designing of instructional activities during the year and determining whether school will or will not be in session. The Yearly Master Calendar records the important school events for the entire year, as well as dates for them that have been established two or three years in advance. Consequently, the Master Calendar has considerable value in reducing the conflicts and duplications which might arise among competing activities, programs or organizations. The instructional program of the school should serve as a foundation for constructing the calendar which, in turn, should include dates relating to both student and community activities. Because larger school units require more complex calendars, various types of calendars are often utilized by schools to organize their total curricular program.

THE MASTER CALENDAR

The Master Control Calendar or Yearly School Calendar usually provides a panoramic registry of the activities—both instructional and noninstructional—over a period of three years. The current year's calendar exerts control over the ongoing school session, while the following two years identify those future dates that have already been determined. These dates might include state and national holidays, the beginning and ending of school, and, at the secondary level, interscholastic athletic contracts which often extend over a two- or three-year period.

Anderson and Van Dyke have compiled the following list of items that are generally included in a school calendar:

1. Dates of opening and closing the school year.

2. Schedule of events for the first week of school.

3. Schedule of events for the closing days of school, including commencement and senior class events.

4. Recesses for holidays, teacher conventions, and such traditional community affairs as may be considered by the board of education to be of sufficient importance.

5. Local staff meetings, such as preschool conferences, workshops, system-wide faculty meetings, and regular faculty meetings.

6. Special student activities including:
   a. Major social events.
   b. Athletic contests.
   c. Assemblies.
   d. Dramatic productions.
   e. Speech and forensic events.
   f. Music concerts and productions.
   g. Competitions, such as scholarship exams, state meets, etc.
   h. Student council events, including elections.

7. Dates for examinations and testing programs.

8. Administrative procedures, such as dates for reporting grades to parents, parent conferences, due dates for teachers' reports to the principal, dates for administering supplies and equipment, student registration, American Education Week, and open house observances.

9. Group guidance events, such as career days and special conferences.

10. Community school events, such as PTA meetings, adult education classes, community forums, and concerts.[1]

Priorities.   Establishing a system of priorities may be necessary, if the number of activities to be listed tends to conflict. Bent and McCann have listed what they described as a logical system of priorities for scheduling events on the school calendar.

1. Dates of the opening and closing of school, of vacations during the school year, and any others which are established by the board of education.

2. Dates established by regional, state, or other authorities beyond the school system. This includes dates set by regional accrediting associations, state departments of education, the state university, activities associations, and professional organizations in education.

3. Dates established by agreement with other schools. These include dates established for athletic contests by game contracts and other similar agreements.

4. Dates established for the entire high school, such as those for health examinations, commencement, and others.

5. Dates for activities involving large numbers of students, such as career days, class plays, or musical concerts.

6. Dates requested by individual student organizations, small groups of students, or individuals.[2]

Although this list of priorities is concerned primarily with secondary school programs, it is easily adaptable to any school regardless of grade-level organization. For example, if the school unit has a close working relationship with the community, as is often the case in many smaller systems, the list might

---

[1]Lester W. Anderson and Lauren A. Van Dyke, *Secondary School Administration* (Boston: Houghton Mifflin Company, 1963), pp. 184-85. Reprinted by permission of the publisher.

[2]Rudyard K. Bent and Lloyd E. McCann, *Administration of Secondary Schools* (New York: McGraw-Hill Book Company, Inc., 1960), pp. 205-06. Reprinted by permission of the publisher and author.

be altered so that school-related community events would be given as high a priority as the items placed second or third on this list. Another factor to consider whenever a college or university in the community affects a sizable number of personnel and students is the coordination of school and university calendars.

Special attention should be given to the "rush" periods of the school year. The beginning and ending of the school year usually present the most problems with the spring months providing the majority of conflicts. Ovard has suggested that school calendars and schedules reflect a "slow down" period during the spring when the activities become much more numerous. His recommendations call for provisions for "a period when students can concentrate on the completion of their academic programs, and teachers can begin their work of ending school year."[3]

One of the best techniques of planning for future dates is to maintain a daily log of events which can be used as a reference in establishing the dates for similar occasions the following year. A sample log is illustrated in Figure 7.1.

Displaying the Calendar. A number of schools display their master calendars in a window-book format in the central office, thus making it readily available to the students, the faculty, the staff, and the public. A sample display of this type is illustrated in Figure 7.2.

Special calendar dates and even monthly calendars might well be attached to the teachers' daily or weekly bulletins thereby reminding them of upcoming events enabling them to schedule both their professional and personal activities around these events. Further information concerning the activity scheduled might include the names of the individuals sponsoring a specific event. In some instances, the maintenance staff on duty are also listed in case keys are needed or some mishap occurs. Figure 7.3 depicts information that might be included in the calendar.

---

[3]Glen F. Ovard, *Administration of the Changing Secondary School* (New York: The Macmillan Company, 1966), p. 148. Copyright © 1966 by Glen F. Ovard. Reprinted by permission of the publisher and the author.

October 2	Curriculum consultants in building to discuss and assist with reading program.
October 4	First Thursday each month is the elementary principals' meeting date throughout the year.
October 5	Student teacher orientation.
October 10	School pictures taken today. Second Wednesday each school month is the elementary principals' dinner meeting.
October 15	Safety assembly with the city police.
October 16	Psychological testing program begun and continued according to schedule throughout the year.
October 18	P.T.A. executive board meeting (meet each calendar month on approximately same date). Supervision and accounting of fire drill required each school month.
October 30	P.T.A. meeting and monthly thereafter except for November and June.
November 7	All report cards completed except for attendance and turned into office for inspection.
November 13	Distribute cards to students.
November 16	Host Philharmonic Orchestra group on stage in assembly for grades 4, 5, and 6.

FIGURE 7.1. Sample Taken from Elementary Principal's Log.

OTHER TYPES OF CALENDARS

Warning Calendars. Many principals use warning calendars to remind faculty of due dates for reports, assignments, special projects, and student evaluations. These calendars often include beginning dates, progress dates, and a final date. Some principals use a checklist format to assist individuals in keeping these deadlines in mind.

Departmental, Grade-Level, and Team-Unit Calendars. Each operating subunit within the school may desire to organize a calendar of its particular activities. Care should be taken, how-

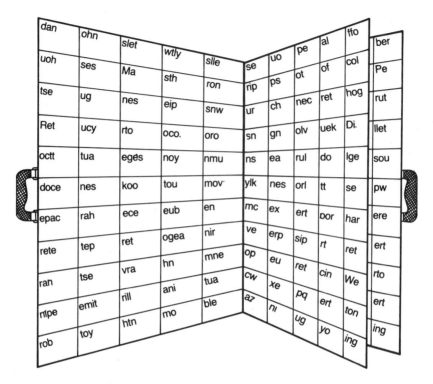

Figure 7.2. Illustration of a Book-Form Master Calendar.

ever, that these calendars be coordinated with the Master Sheet in the principal's office.

Activities Calendar. The activities calendar is of particular value to those schools which have a great number of extra-class activities. Coordination of these activities is a necessity in main-

Thursday, March 12, 19___

7:30 p.m. School Awards

Gym

Mr. Brown: SS 103

(Mr. Jones: maintenance.

Boiler Rm. #5)

Figure 7.3. Item from School Calendar.

taining the proper flow of information. A large secondary school may be conducting debate, music, intramural athletics, various club meetings, and athletic contests all in one day. The athletic director or whoever is responsible for the athletic program should maintain a minimum three-year schedule which is available to the control calendar at all times. Any changes in schedule should be reported immediately to the principal's office.

Building and Room-Use Calendar.   The numerous student activities and increasing demands for use of schools by the public requires the maintenance of a realistic building-use schedule. Whether this schedule is a part of the Master Control Calendar or a separate chart coordinated with the office, the control record depends in part upon the state of the campus and the number of buildings available. This calendar should be made available to the school's maintenance crew.

RESPONSIBILITY

The final responsibility for the administration of the Master Control Calendar resides with the principal. Although he does not control all the dates that must be scheduled, he still has the final responsibility to see that these deadlines are applied or met. Nonetheless, the principal can call on others for assistance. In larger schools a calendar committee composed of administrators, counselors, faculty and students meets regularly to establish priorities on calendar requests. The actual administration of the control calendar is then left to a capable secretary, an administrative officer, or a teaching staff member with released time to perform this duty. It appears that utilization of a capable secretary would be the most effective pattern.

In smaller schools, and, particularly, at the elementary level, the principal or teaching principal coordinates the calendar. In some instances an assistant principal or an individual teacher is assigned this responsibility. Here, again, a capable secretary could well perform this task, freeing other personnel to concentrate on their areas of preparation.

The monthly or weekly calendars should also be color coded (i.e., use specified paper colors for printing each schedule). Thus, when a teacher sees a blue sheet, he knows that this is the Master Schedule for the semester or year. A green sheet could indicate the weekly or monthly calendar. A yellow sheet might signify one of the other types of calendar discussed in this chapter. A sample monthly calendar for a junior high school is depicted in Figure 7.4.

May

    1   Election Assembly — 1st period

    2   Student Body elections — 1st period

    3   Bermuda Day — Dance 2:15 to 4:00 p.m.

    4   Student Council party — Lake Mead

    8   Fashion Show — Home Ec. Department

   10   Faculty Assembly — 6th and 7th periods

13 - 17   Exams

   16   "Playroom" — 7:30 p.m. (Speech Department)

   16   School Board meeting at Jim Bridger
          Jr. High School; Dinner served by Home Ec.
          Department — 7:30 p.m.

FIGURE 7.4. Portion of a Junior High School Monthly Calendar. (Reprinted by courtesy of Von Tobel Junior High School, Clark County School District, Las Vegas, Nevada.)

The school calendar plays a surprisingly important role in the effective management of a school program. It can be an effective communication instrument and morale booster. The calendar, along with the schedule, provides the framework of operations; it organizes time and permits teaching and learning to occur. Theoretically, the ideal calendar makes a significant contribution by allocating and preserving the "time to teach."

QUESTIONS AND SUGGESTIONS FOR STUDY

1. Examine the school calendar in your district or in those districts that are nearby. Identify the different types of calendars. Who is responsible for administering them? How are priorities determined?

2. Develop a master calendar for your school. Describe how you would communicate this information to the students, faculty, and community.

3. What dates on the school calendar are controlled by the principal? Which events cannot be changed?

SELECTED REFERENCES

Bent, Rudyard K., and McCann, Lloyd E. *Administration of Secondary Schools.* New York: McGraw-Hill Book Co., 1960, pp. 204-06.

Linder, Ivan H., and Gunn, Henry M. *Secondary School Administration.* Columbus, Ohio: Charles E. Merrill Publishing Co., 1963, p. 51.

Ovard, Glen F. *Administration of the Changing Secondary School.* New York: The Macmillan Co., 1966, pp. 147-48.

Chapter Eight

Programming the
Extended School Year

The terms *all-year school, year-round school, summer school,* and *extended-year school* have been used interchangeably to identify various programs for the extension of the traditional 180-day school year. However, operational patterns of these programs vary considerably, as do their philosophical and behavioral objectives. However, these various programs primarily center around opportunities for student acceleration, enrichment and/or remediation; the economic advantages of year-round utilization of facilities; and provision for flexibility within the instructional program.

The longer school year is certainly not a new concept. As early as 1840, a few city school districts in the United States conducted programs throughout the entire year. In rural areas, however, the sessions were brief because students were needed for work on the farm. By 1915, a majority of the nation's schools operated on a nine or ten month calendar—the calendar which has remained in some form as the norm throughout our educational system since that time.

In 1925, thirteen different schools across the nation attempted to implement some type of extended-school-year plan, primarily for economic reasons. By the beginning of the depression, all of these plans had been abandoned because of administrative problems, parental objections to the staggered vacation periods, or because expected economies had not been realized.

In the late 1940's and early 1950's the extended-year school programs received another impetus. Generally economical in nature, these programs were also encouraged because of the changes needed to meet new curriculum innovations in the schools.

Advantages and Disadvantages

Current supporters of the year-round school believe that the educational needs of citizens living in today's complex and changing society can scarcely be met with educational programs based on the 180-day school year. Advanced technology and a greater competition for jobs at all levels have created new occupations requiring greater knowledge and higher-level skills requiring more specialization. As a consequence, more pupils must be provided with more and better education. These challenges can be met, at least in part, through a comprehensive, well-implemented full-year educational program.

Steven A. Knezevich summarizes some of the advantages for extending the school year in this manner:

1. It would allow fuller utilization of school-plant facilities and possibly forestall the need for new school construction.
2. It would reduce certain unit costs of operation, such as fixed charges and administration.
3. It would utilize the staff more fully.
4. It would keep urban youngsters engaged in constructive programs during the summer.
5. It would permit moving some non-academic experiences, such as driver education and typing, to the summer leaving more time for academic subjects during the rest of the year.
6. It would permit use of school facilities for the professional growth and development of teachers.[1]

Some disadvantages have become apparent as schools attempted to incorporate various forms of the extended-school-

---

[1]Steven J. Knezevich, *Administration of Public Education* (New York; Harper and Brother, Publishers, 1969) p. 396. Reprinted by permission of the publisher.

year plans. Among the concerns that have been expressed are: problems in balancing class loads to tie in with traditional vacation patterns; the problem of smaller schools which often cannot fully schedule courses for the entire year; the inevitability of higher building and maintenance costs, at least initially, because of the need to install air conditioning and to make maintenance a year-round project; the extension of transportation costs; the necessity of greater salary expenditures for all personnel is required; the curtailing or limitation of student activities of all kinds.

The implications for maintaining a year-round calendar and schedule under any extended-year program are obvious. More time would need to be spent in the management details of the calendar itself, and scheduling would become a full-time activity. The concepts and principles discussed in previous chapters would still apply, although the function itself would need to be duplicated and/or operated continuously because of the nature of the program. One consequence would be that full-time personnel would need to be provided to complete these assignments, if they were available initially. In addition, the unlimited opportunities to utilize new data processing concepts in a continuous calendar program would necessitate trained management personnel to implement these schedules.

TYPES OF EXTENDED-YEAR PLANS

The 1970 publication *9+, The Year-Round School* by the American Association of School Administrators briefly describes five basic types of plans for extending the school year. These include Staggered Quarter for All, A Full 48-Week School Year for All, A Voluntary Summer Program, A Summer Program for Professional Personnel and a relatively new plan, The Multiple Trails Program.[2]

The following terms will be used in this chapter to identify the various extended-school-year programs. The classifications

---

[2]American Association of School Administrators, *9+, The Year-Round School* (Washington, D.C.: American Association of School Administrators, 1970), pp. 10-11. Reprinted by permission of the publisher.

have been revised somewhat to incorporate very recent adaptations of these plans.

1. The Four Quarter Plan
   1.1   Standard four quarter
   1.2   Quadrimester
   1.3   Staggered quarter

2. The Trimester
   2.1   Standard Trimester
   2.2   Split Trimester

3. Summer School Program
   3.1   Extension of regular year (standard) (voluntary)
   3.2   Modified summer program

4. The Multiple Trails Program

5. The 45-15 Plan

6. Other Combinations
   6.1   Continuous progress plan
   6.2   Split semester plan

The Four Quarter Plan

The Standard Quarter Plan.   Standard quarter patterns are based upon division of the forty-eight-week school year into four quarters or quadrimesters ranging from fifty-one to sixty days in length. Class periods are lengthened to parallel the instructional time of traditional programs. With this plan, students may complete five years of work in three, depending upon the grade-level organization of the unit or the policy of the school district involved. Since a one quarter summer vacation is included, full attendance through all quarters is not mandatory.

A specific example of the quarter plan is the program developed in Fulton County, Georgia (The Atlanta Plan). According to Knezevich:

> ... this plan prepared the traditional nine-month school structure, the carnegie unit credit, the concept of the totally sequential

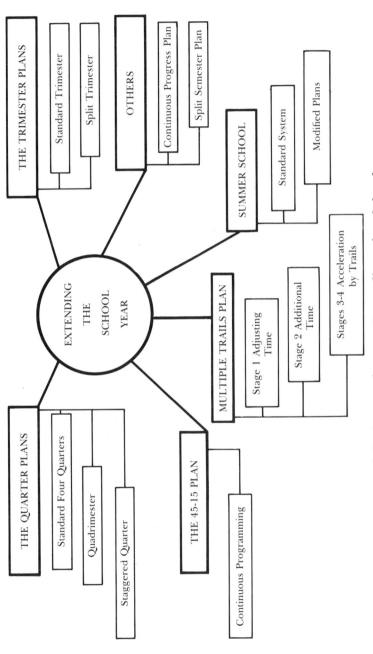

FIGURE 8.1. Approaches to Extending the School Year.

179

curriculum, and the practice of scheduling student into a master schedule one time each year.[3]

The prime purpose of this particular program was to improve educational opportunities and not just to save money. Fringe benefits of the experiment provided additional classroom space as well as special opportunities for both the gifted and the slow learner to advance at a faster pace.

The Quadrimester Plan. Generally, the quadrimester program differs from a majority of the four-quarter plans in that the student must continue *through the full 200* plus days of attendance (i.e., through a mandatory program). In some cases, an *E* or *enrichment* term is added for either the accelerated student or the slow learner who either needs remedial work or to repeat a course. (Ramifications of the *E* term will be discussed later in this chapter.)

A New York State Department of Education report provides examples of what might happen to students in differing programs and in varying flow patterns within a quadrimester plan.

Figure 8.3 depicts a comparison of regular and extended year calendars.

Figure 8.3 provides a schematic diagram of the various extended school year designs.

A student flow pattern in a Five-Year Quadrimester Plan is illustrated in Figure 8.6. A Four Year Flow Plan is illustrated in Figure 8.7.

In planning for the quadrimester calendar, administrators should consider the curriculum-time goals involved. For example, the quadrimester design may be for a five-year program to be completed in four, for a four-year program to be completed in three, for a three-year program to be completed in two, or for variations of any flow pattern designed to meet the needs of each district's goals.

Although most extended year plans were primarily designed for secondary schools, the quadrimester plan lends itself readily to elementary programs. Figure 8.8 illustrates a model elemen-

---

[3]Steven J. Knezevich, p. 394.

1. Pupils completing a course at the end of
   the third quadrimester begin new courses
   in the fourth quadrimester which carry
   over into the next school year.

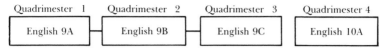

2. Pupils completing a course at the end of
   the second quadrimester begin a new
   course in the third quadrimester. It may
   be completed in the first quadrimester of
   the following year or it may be completed
   during the same calendar year through
   double-period scheduling for one or both
   of the ensuing quadrimesters.

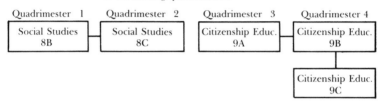

3. Pupils may elect new courses which have
   been prepared as one- or two-quadrimes-
   ter courses.

4. Pupils who work slowly may receive more
   instructional time through taking courses
   which have been broken up into shorter
   learning units or segments, to allow pupils
   to progress at a slower pace. Through the
   use of the "E" terms, it is possible to offer
   such courses in four quadrimesters instead of three (World History, Biology,
   Chemistry, etc.).

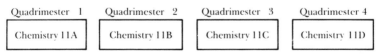

FIGURE 8.2[4]

[4]George I. Thomas, *Extended School Year Designs* (New York: State Board of Education, 1966), p. 5. Reprinted by permission of the publisher.

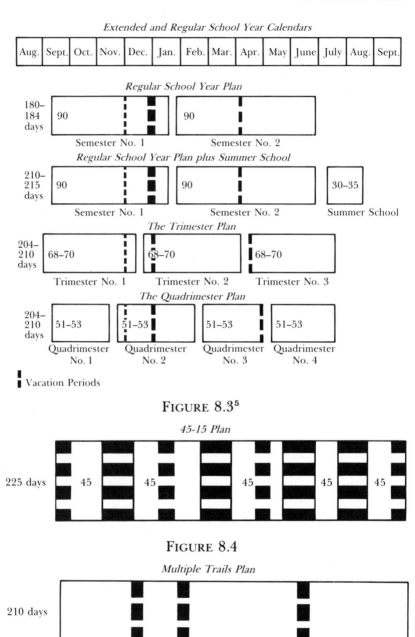

Extended and Regular School Year Calendars

FIGURE 8.3[5]

45-15 Plan

FIGURE 8.4

Multiple Trails Plan

FIGURE 8.5

[5]Thomas, p. 5.

Student Flow Pattern in a Five-Year Quadrimester Plan

FIGURE 8.6[6]

tary school flow pattern as reported in the New York State Board of Education report regarding the extended school year.

The Staggered Quarter Plan. The staggered quarter plan as described in the AASA publication on the year-round school is organized so that a different group of students is on vacation during each quarter. An illustration of how a basic schedule under this system might look appears in Figure 8.9. Generally the enrollment in each of these groups needs to be approximately equal to provide the appropriate courses and to allow for the flexibility required by electives.

The Trimester

Standard Trimester. The concept of the regular trimester plan divides the school year into three trimesters of approximately sixty-five to seventy-five days. These may be divided by brief vacation periods plus the normal holidays, or they can be so arranged as to leave only registration and planning days off between trimesters, thereby utilizing only the normal state and

[6]Thomas, p. 54.

The Four-Year Quadrimester Flow Pattern

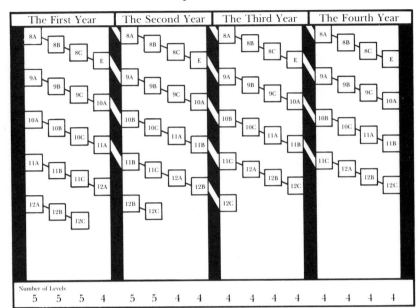

The reduction in school enrollment takes place at the end of the ninth quadrimester. At this time, the new flow pattern becomes permanent and the
five-level school reduces to four levels.

Figure 8.7[7]

national holidays for vacation periods. As a consequence of the
occurrence of these holidays within the calendar, some trimesters would be longer than others in terms of actual class days.

Split Trimester.   The split trimester differs from the standard
trimester in that it compromises the regular semester pattern
with that of the more traditional summer schools. The school
year is extended by adding a third time unit, or trimester, which
is split into two portions—one based on mandatory attendance
and one on voluntary enrollment or, in some instances, partially
optional enrollment. Figure 8.10 presents an example.

Trimester 3A or 3B in the illustration may be reversed or duplicated. Students then may select their vacation in either 3A or 3B.
Similar patterns may be used to develop split quadrimester.
Figure 8.11 illustrates a program of a student who is attending
a split trimester school for fourteen out of fifteen trimesters.

---

[7] Ibid., p. 58.

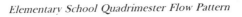

Elementary School Quadrimester Flow Pattern

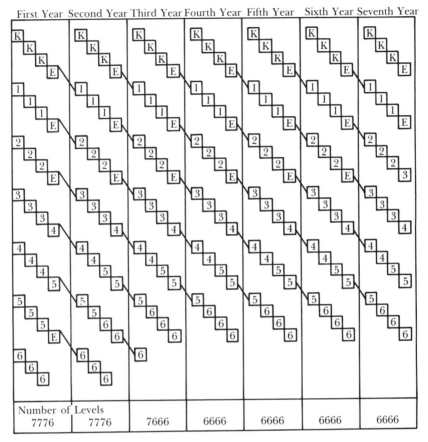

FIGURE 8.8[8]

The E Term Concept

The *E* term was devised to assist with the problem of balancing enrollments during the lighter sessions of a quadrimester or trimester plan. In general, the letter *E* refers to a variety of concepts. Among these are *extra* education, *extended* time, *enrichment* opportunities, and, in a few cases, *excellence* in education.

---

[8]Thomas, p. 60.

	12 weeks	12 weeks	12 weeks	12 weeks
Group A	Vacation			
Group B		Vacation		
Group C			Vacation	
Group D				Vacation

Figure 8.9[9]

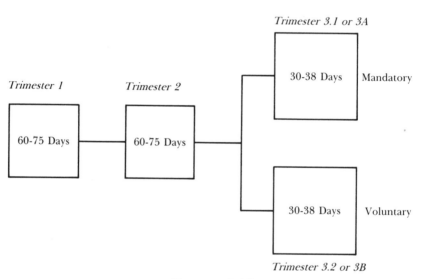

Figure 8.10

Operationally, the *E* phase may be inserted between quad-rimesters or trimesters to help a student complete his work earlier, receive additional help, or broaden and enrich his curriculum. For example, an eighth-grade student with a reading problem could enroll in a special *E* term to correct this deficiency and then move into the appropriate class level during the next calendar unit. These extended programs provide the

[9]American Association of School Administrators, p. 12.

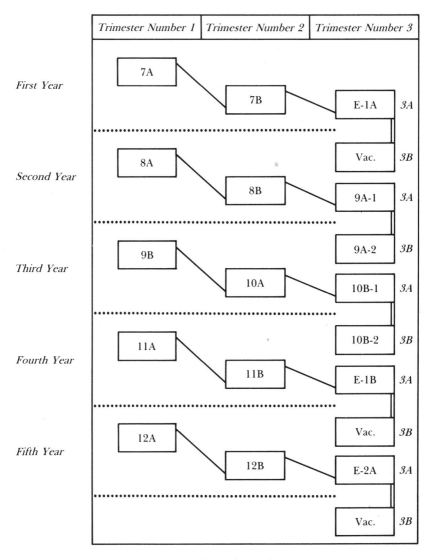

*Trimester Session 3A is mandatory, but
Trimester Session 3B is partially optional.

FIGURE 8.11[10]

---

[10]Thomas, George I., p. 92.

needed extra time for diagnosis and remediation as well as for exploration and supplementation. *E* terms may also be used as elective vacation periods.

Summer School Programs

Extension of the Regular Year (Standard-Voluntary). This format for extending the school year has been the most predominate pattern followed across the nation. Originally designed to assist the slow learner, it recently has come to include enrichment and special programs as well. These "summer schools" generally begin one to two weeks after the regular year ends and last from five to eight weeks. Since all too often they are self-supporting, schools sometimes have been forced to cancel special courses because student enrollments were too low, thus defeating the purpose of the course or project itself. Initially, such programs require the same scheduling procedures as utilized in standard programs.

Modified Summer Programs. One form of modified summer program is described in the AASA publication on the year-round school. The classification is called *Summer Programs for Professional Personnel* and, in general, operates as follows:

1. Teachers are employed on a twelve-month basis with forty-eight work-weeks and four weeks of vacation.
2. Children attend school for the traditional thirty-six to forty weeks.
3. Teachers, together with administrators and supervisors in the district, are engaged in instructional and curriculum planning during the twelve summer weeks when children are not in school. They review instructional fields and revise the curriculum content in science, geography, economics, government, and other segments of the program to bring it up-to-date; they think through carefully instructional methods in light of the latest educational research findings; they survey the different instructional materials and equipment that are continuously coming onto the market; and they review evaluative procedures and promotion policies.
4. The school board, supervisors, principals, teachers, administrators, and leaders of various lay organizations in the community join with the superintendent in developing a plan of

work. Together they decide what needs to be done and how to do it. Wide publicity in the school district is given to the program so that everyone has a chance to understand the purposes and nature of this part of the community school program. A vital functional program of this kind varies considerably from year to year. Some teachers may spend the time in advanced study at a college or university; others will be engaged in a workshop in the local school district, actually preparing materials for use during the next school year. Other teachers may spend the time in a professional organization, in a business establishment, in the research laboratory of an industrial plant, on a nature study expedition, or in visiting foreign countries for the purpose of getting first-hand acquaintance with various aspects of cultural development. The program is flexible enough to make use of numerous kinds of experiences and resources, but through careful planning all efforts are directed to the common purpose of bringing life and vitality into the instructional program.

5. There is no rigid requirement that every teacher participate in the 12-week summer program of professional improvement. Exceptions are made when hardships or extreme difficulties are imposed on individual teachers. Maintaining the physical and emotional well-being of every member of the teaching staff is a prime function of this program, and therefore, the program avoids becoming entrapped in a rigid pattern that defeats this very purpose.[11]

Other modified forms schedule summer school programs from early June through early August, either with or without a break between these dates (i.e., a split summer session). In essence, this practice could become a trimester but, operationally and organizationally, it is an extension of the regular school year through the summer.

The Multiple Trails Program[12]

This plan is designed to spread the normal year's instruction time over a 210-day year with classes meeting less often and for shorter periods of time than under the traditional system. A July or August vacation is scheduled in addition to the eleven month

---

[11]American Association of School Administrators, p. 18-19.
[12]American Association of School Administrators, pp. 21-22.

school year. Normal holidays during the academic year are also included.

Modules (modular scheduling) or time serve as the basis for restructuring the schedules, and implementation occurs in four stages. The purpose of *stage one* is to adjust student-faculty schedules by reducing contact time by approximately 25 percent. During *stage two,* released pupil time may be used for acceleration. In *stages three* and *four,* the additional classroom space made available and the increased pupil-teacher time for remediation, enrichment, and work experience are all incorporated into the year long plan.

The 45-15 Plan.   A school calendar that sends pupils home for vacations of at least fifteen days after every forty-five days of school is the concept behind this new experimental extended school year project. The basic pattern is to stagger four groups and to alternate programs accordingly. As a consequence, 25 percent of the pupils are always on vacation.

The Valley View Elementary School District 96, serving over 700 elementary schools in the villages of Romeoville and Bolingbrook, Illinois, has found the 45-15 plan to offer a solution to its financial and space problems. School officials felt that additional time and space was successfully purchased to meet the rapidly expanding school population which confronted their area. They also have experienced greater curricular flexibility, increased average and daily attendance, and the development of an increased acceptability toward innovation and change.

The communities have had major adjustments to make, however, in several instances. Different children from the same families are home at different times because of the staggered vacations; the summer recreation programs have dwindled; church schools have been forced to revise their summer plans; and a few of the local stores have reported that the incidence of increased shoplifting is no longer confined to the summer months.

The 45-15 Plan was initially implemented as follows: One fourth of the students attend school for forty-five days. On the sixteenth day of this period, a second group would enter. On the thirty-first day, a third group would enter. On the forty-sixth day, Group 1 would go on vacation and Group 4 would replace them. Fifteen days later the cycle would start all over again as depicted in the following diagram.

Cycling of Groups Under the 45-15 Plan

Groups   0   15   30   45   60   75

(1   2   3   4)

1 _____ 4 _____ 90 ____
                                        (start second
      2 _____ A   quarter or 45 days)   (105)____

            3 _____

A copy of the Valley View 45-15 calendar for the 1971 year appears in Figure 8.12. Numerous other 45-15 plans are presently in effect across the nation. Some successful current programs are the Hayward, California, Elementary District: the elementary schools of Mora, Minnesota: and some elementary schools within the huge Chicago system which are now experimenting with this calendar.

CHARACTERISTICS OF EXTENDED SCHOOL YEAR DESIGNS

A task force report from the Clark County Schools in Las Vegas, Nevada, has charted the characteristics of certain selected extended school year designs. This summarization is reproduced in Figure 7.

The task force also developed some general criteria for evaluation of the programs to select the one best suited to their area. This portion of that report follows:

EXTENDED-SCHOOL-YEAR CRITERIA FOR EVALUATION OF PROGRAMS

A. *Purposes to be Served*

Plans are available to do most anything a school district would like to do, but the District must decide what it is it wants to

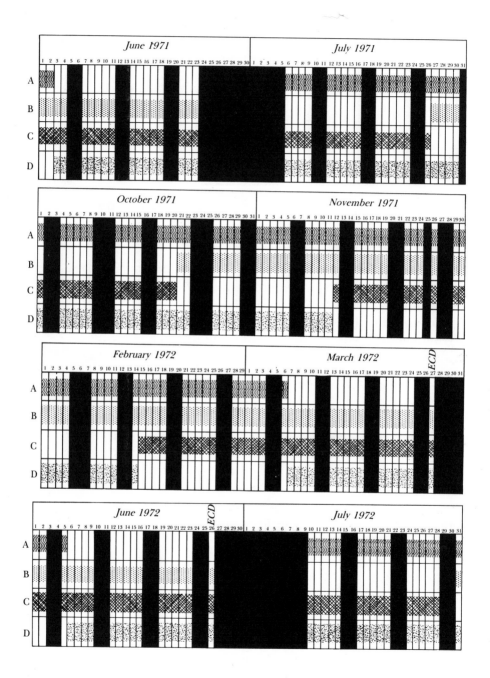

192

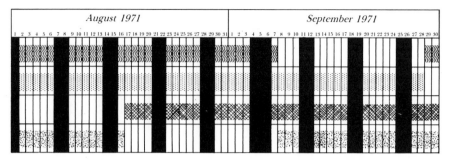

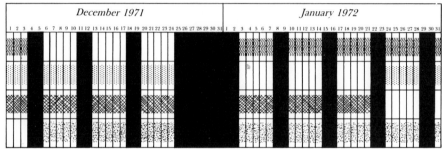

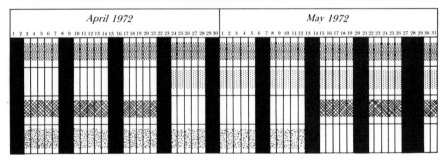

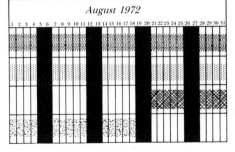

FIGURE 8.12. Pupil Calendar—Valley View 45-15

Continuous School Year Plan (Developed by Research and Development Office Valley View School District #96, Lockport, Illinois. Copyright c 1971 by Valley View School District #96. Reprinted by permission of the Clark County School District).

| Group A | | Group C | |
| Group B | | Group D | |

ECD—Emergency Closing Day

Characteristic	The Continuous School Year Plan	The Two Semester plus Modified Summer School Plan	The Trimester Plan of School Organization	The Quadrimester Plan of School Organization	The Extended K to 12 Plan of School Organization
Length of the Extended Year	203 to 216 days	Regular 180 days plus 35 to 40 day summer segment	204 to 225 days	204 to 220 days	204 to 225 days
Length of the School Day	Normal hrs. Sept.-June; 4 to 4½ hrs. July or August	Normal hrs. Sept.-June; 3½-4 hrs. July or August	Normal hrs. Sept.-June; 4 to 4½ hrs. July or August	Normal hrs. Sept.-June; 4 to 4½ hrs. July or August	Normal school days
Divisions in School Year	None	Two 90 day semesters plus a 36 to 40 day summer segment	Three 70 to 75 day trimesters	Four continuous quadrimesters	None in elementary school 3 or 4 in secondary school
Grade Levels Included	K to 6, 1 to 6 or 1 to 8	7 to 12, 8 to 12, or 1 to 8	7 to 12, 8 to 12 or 9 to 12	7 to 12, or K to 6 8 to 12, 9 to 12	K to 12
Time Required to Effect Savings in Classrooms, Teachers and Dollars	5 to 6 years	3 yrs. for gr. 9 to 12 5 yrs. for gr. 7 to 12	1 to 1½ years	2 to 2¼ years	1⅓ years to 2¼ years
Time Required to Become Self-Sustaining	5 to 6 years	5 years	Self-sustaining after first adjustment year	After 1 yr. in 3 and 4 yr. quadrimester, after 2nd yr. in 5 yr. quadrimester	May become self-sustaining in second year
Vacations Beyond Normal Christmas and Spring Recess	6 to 7 weeks	4 weeks	4 to 7 weeks	4 to 7 weeks	4 to 7 weeks

Number of "E" Terms	No "E" term equivalent	None	3 in 5 yr. plan 2 in 4 yr. plan 1 in 3 yr. plan	2 in 5 yr. plan 1 in 4 yr. plan 0 in 3 yr. plan	Elementary pupils may accumulate 220 to 280 extra days of schooling with secondary pupils having 2-3 "E" terms
Advantages	Pupils have fewer teacher changes. Pupils have more time in their formative years to master skills required for success in later years. The program is built on a philosophy that continuous progress will become a reality	Programs are more than remedial. Summer segment is integrated with regular school yr. so pupils are free to take new or advanced courses in the regular school year. Gives more continuity to entire school program	Classrooms, special areas and teachers are released in 1⅓ yrs. Pupils have up to 3 extra "E" terms. Pupils can use options for work experience or to enter college at other than normal September entry. Reduces dropout rate	Classrooms, special areas and teachers are released in 2 to 2¼ years. Pupils have up to 2 "E" terms. Pupils can use options for work experience or to enter college at other than normal September entry. Reduces dropout rate	Provides more educational opportunities to all types of pupils. Dropout rate reduced. Releases classrooms, special areas, and number of instructors required in 1⅓ to 2¼ years. Pupils can use options to obtain work experience or to enter college at other than normal Sept. entry. Keeps all children on same school calendar.

FIGURE 8.13. Characteristics of Selected Extended-School-Year Designs[13]

[13]Unpublished Task Force Report on the Extended School Year. Clark County School District, Las Vegas, Nevada, 1970.

achieve. It may be impossible to find a single plan for an extended school year which would meet all desirable objectives.

B. *Economic Conditions*

1. Economy cannot be the only reason for a year-round program. The quality of the educational program must also be improved or it will not succeed. If students and parents see no personal advantage, an emotional controversy could arise which would doom any program providing solely an economic advantage.
2. If the quality of the educational program is improved and the program made relevant it will cost more money. If there is not improvement in the educational program, then it is not worth the expenditure of additional public funds.
3. Financing must be the same as the regular portion of the year with state support.

C. *Educational Factors*

1. Acceleration—provision must be made to allow students the opportunity to reduce the amount of time required to graduate from high school.
2. Enrichment—opportunity to participate in activities for which there is insufficient time during the regular school year must be provided.
3. Remediation—a student should be able to repeat courses failed or to obtain special help in areas needed.

D. *Curriculum*

1. Continuous progress for the individual must be a part of the on-going program. A traditional curriculum cannot be placed into an extended year.
2. The program must be relevant to student needs.
3. Unless there is willingness for major curriculum innovation, the extended school year should not be attempted.

E. *Community*

1. The extended school year must be mandatory as is the regular school year. A voluntary program is doomed to failure through lack of support.

2. The particular extended school year plan must be specific for a particular community. The following items must be taken into consideration:
   a. The type occupational structure of parents and the extent to which it is seasonal in nature.
   b. Community vacation patterns.
   c. Scheduling of major athletic events.
   d. The extreme summer heat conditions and its limiting effect upon activities outside air-conditioned classrooms.
   e. Tourist trade and the 24-hour nature of Las Vegas.
   f. The extent to which school curricular offerings are correlated with the vocational needs of the community.
   g. Family living patterns such as work schedules, number of working parents, etc.

F. *Professional Staff Utilization*

1. Does the extended school year allow for more students to interact with teachers having unique talents?
2. The extended school year should provide greater opportunity for teacher involvement in curriculum development.
3. Professional growth opportunities for teachers must be increased through greater flexibility as to times of attendance at universities.[14]

EXAMPLES OF EXTENDED YEAR PLANS

The Atlanta Plan-A Voluntary Quarter Plan

In the fall of 1968 a voluntary quarter plan was initiated in the twenty-six Atlanta high schools. The prime motivational purpose of this plan was to reorganize the high school calendar so that year-round educational opportunities could be developed and more flexible and viable programs realized. A potential by-product would be some relief for overcrowded school facilities.

Two years of intensive planning preceded actual implementation of the program. Courses were designed to be autonomous (i.e., with the least possible dependence upon sequence), and

---

[14]Ibid.

much greater variety of quarter courses were also designed based upon pupil needs.

The school year was divided into three quarters of fifty-nine days each and one summer quarter of fifty-three days. All sessions operate on a full day in each quarter. Since state aid does not exceed the legal 190-day minimum Foundation Program in Georgia, the additional funds come from local funds (tuition) and from certain federally funded projects.

Teachers salaries are on an index schedule based on the 190-day employment regulation. No one is required to work the summer quarter but those who do are paid at the same rate as the previous quarters, thus providing for flexibility in scheduling, greater involvement of teachers in the counseling program, in-service programs for teachers.

Evaluation course construction and funding have been major concerns in implementing this program. Conversion tables for changing quarter hours to Carnegie units also were developed. Perhaps one of the single major problems was the location of single-concept materials and textbooks since most publications are written on a longer unit-concept basis.

The Atlanta Program is currently a voluntary program—in 1971, 11,666 of 43,466 (35.5 percent) of the students participated in the plan. These students took an average of 3.725 subjects per pupil. Community support has been favorable since it was made clear that students could select the quarters they would attend. The trend since 1969 has been a positive one in Atlanta—a voluntary program which appears to be working.

The 45-15 Plan-Valley View School District

The Valley View (Elementary K-8) School District #96, Lockport, Illinois, implemented its mandatory 45-15 plan on June 30, 1970. As described earlier in this report, this plan involved students attending school for forty-five days (nine weeks) and then being off for fifteen days (three weeks). Three-fourths of the students are in school all of the time while the remaining fourth is on vacation.

The district covers forty square miles in Will County, which is adjacent to Cook County (Chicago) in northeastern Illinois.

Currently over 6,800 students are enrolled, and the projection of a potential 20,000 by 1980 has been made. Assessed valuation per student has decreased from $162,098 in 1953 to $21,440 in 1967–70. Sixty-seven percent of all revenues come from local tax dollars.

The prime purpose of this plan was to save money and to provide additional classroom space. Consequent factors have been a revised, and more flexible curriculum and a belief that the quality of education has increased.

Thus far, the implementation of this plan has resulted in saving the construction costs of seventy-six equipped class-rooms. 1972–1979 Projected Building Programs indicate the following savings under the 45-15 Plan.

	Traditional Year	45-15 Plan	Difference
New Junior High Schools	2	2	
New Elementary Schools	6	3	
Total Cost of Building	$11,080,000	$7,540,000	$3,540,000
Interest Paid on New Building Bonds during Period	2,459,574	1,416,108	1,043,465
Principal Retired during Period	1,553,686	880,051	673,634
Debt Outstanding at End of Period	9,526,313	6,659,948	2,866,365

FIGURE 8-14[15]

Figure 10 indicates cost per pupil savings as reported by the Valley View study.

The major problem was community approval, but this diffi-culty has been resolved to a large extent. An extensive program of information dissemination was developed before any attempt was made to implement the plan. Although there still remain problems of community acceptance, staffing, and some technical aspects, the school officials feel that their 45-15 plan has met

[15] *Planning A Year-Round School Operation, Final Report,* Project No. 0-0011, U.S. Office of Education, Bureau of Research (Lockport, Illinois: Valley View School District, January, 1971), p. 141.

	Valley View 1969-70 (Enrollment 5,580)		Valley View under 45-15 Plan (7,440 enrollment)[1]	
	Total	Per Pupil	Total	Per Pupil
Administration	$ 208,000	$ 37.27	$ 238,000[2]	$ 31.98
Instruction	2,859,300	512.42	3,800,000[3]	510.75
Health	34,200	6.13	45,600	6.13
Operation	389,900	69.87	500,000[4]	67.20
Maintenance	34,100	6.11	40,000[5]	5.38
Fixed charges	163,200	29.25	217,600	29.25
Other (except food)	45,100	8.08	60,000	8.06
Net Current	$3,733,800	$669.14	$4,901,200	$658.75
Transportation	296,400	53.12	390,000[6]	52.42
Debt service	488,400	87.53	488,400[7]	65.65
Capital outlay	(766,000)	(137.27)	(766,000)[8]	(102.96)
	$ 784,800	$140.65	$ 878,400	$118.06
Total	$4,518,600	$809.78	$5,779,600	$776.82

[1]Assumes enrollment expanded one-third and no inflation.
[2]Assumes two additional administrators, one to help with scheduling.
[3]Assumes some savings in small equipment and materials.
[4]Assumes janitors work less hours during vacation periods.
[5]Assumes some increase in repairs but not proportionately.
[6]Assumes some savings in equipment but this may be optimistic because extended routes may wipe out this difference.
[7]Actually interest would drop a bit each year as principal was paid off.
[8]An expenditure but not chargeable because it is reflected already through debt retirement.

Figure 8.15.[16] Cost per Pupil on Two Bases of Comparison (Figures rounded to $100)

with measureable success and plan to continue it at Valley View #96.

The Hayward Unified Schools Four-Quarter Plan

The California legislature recently granted a five-year extension (AB 1691) of the *compulsory* year-round school that has been under way in one elementary unit in the Hayward Unified School District since 1968. The experimental plan was orginally

---

[16]*Planning a Year-Round School Operation*, p. 140.

funded under a Title III ESEA project, as was the Valley View 45-15 plan in Illinois.

An early feasibility study recently completed, involving written surveys, open meetings, a newspaper survey, and a final written questionnaire, indicated eighty percent acceptance of the compulsory plan. Preliminary investigation also indicated that significant gains were made in reading and mathematics when scores were compared with a control school on the traditional plan.

The school year consists of four quarters of approximately fifty days each, with three weeks between quarters. One week of each break is utilized for parent conferences, teacher in-service programs, and planning. Because of the nature of the Park School program, the District's curriculum framework had to be modified to meet special needs of the year-round school. All classes of the school are nongraded, and pupils are placed in classes on basis of total need as determined by the teachers.

Summary results of the most recent study of the project indicate the following:

Student Achievement—Reading and Mathematics: The Park Elementary students performed very well where net achievement gains were compared with the net gain of the comparison school. On the pretest, the comparison school earned consistently higher scores than did the students at Park. However, there was practically no difference in grade achievement levels after one year of operation, thus indicating that the Park pupils generally gained and had caught up with the initially more advanced comparison students.

Acceptance of the Program: The parents of Park Elementary children like, accept, and support the four-quarter system. Seventy-nine percent of the parents answered "yes" when asked if they like the new school year at Park rather than the two semester year. More than half of the parents stated that their children were more highly motivated and that they learned more in the new system.

Students at Park stated that they like the program, and the majority of them do not want the school to return to the former system.

Teachers at Park are generally favorable toward the program. Their acceptance and support is much greater than other teachers not at Park. Teachers not at Park have little information about the program.

Financial Considerations: To make any valid conclusion concerning financial costs on the basis of a one-year study is questionable. However, the data seems to indicate that the costs of operating an additional nineteen days do not materially increase the fixed costs per ADA. The major increases in costs are for certificated salaries. The total cost of operating the Park Program for the nineteen additional instructional days above the regular school year of 175 days was approximately 10 percent.[17]

Other Plans

The Chicago Schools plan to utilize one of the four following plans by September 1972.

1. The Staggered Four-Quarter Plan.
2. The 45-15 Year Round Plan.
3. The 60-20 Day or 12 Week-4 Week Plan.
4. The 8 a.m.-10:00 p.m. Flexible High School Plan (allowing students to work all day and attend school at nights).

A cost analysis study of these proposals (which allows schools the choice of selecting the plan they desire) estimated the following costs:

Additional teachers' salaries	$ 8.1 million
Air Conditioning of twenty of the fifty-four schools under construction	$ 2.1 million
Extra maintenance costs	$14.3 million
Programmer	$ .7 million

The Dade County Quinimester (five-semester plan) was implemented with a $490,000 supplementary budget. The year has been extended to 225 days—cost figures on the program are currently being analyzed.

---

[17] *A Feasibility Study: An Organizational and Curriculum Plan for a Four Quarter Elementary School* (Hayward Unified School District, California, 1969).

Nova High School, Ft. Lauderdale, Florida, is experimenting with various extended-year plans. This practice has been in operation since 1963 when the school opened with a trimester plan. Community pressure for summer vacations, budgeting, teacher certification problems, and lack of legal sanction of the extended school year have forced Nova to move to a modified summer plan somewhat similar to the split trimester.

FACTORS TO CONSIDER FOR IMPLEMENTATION

There are numerous projects relating to the extended year on the drawing boards at this time. Currently there are reportedly over 600 school districts experimenting with one plan or another, and certain factors relative to implementing any year-round plan stand out. Many of these considerations follow:

Effects of the Extended Year on the Pupils

What types of pressures may or may not occur with a continuous education plan?

Does achievement increase?

Does the program allow for all phases of work, enrichment, remediation, and interest?

Is acceleration an important factor in this day and age?

What happens to student activities at school, at home, and in the community?

Effects on the Curriculum

How much curriculum revision will be necessary to adapt to the new schedules?

What effect will the necessary curriculum change have on supplementary materials, textbooks as they are now structured, and current curriculum guides?

Will some schools be forced to adopt an entirely new school program?

How much planning time does the extended year require?

Will curricular changes be made to meet student needs in the new organizational pattern?

Effect on the Teachers

Is the revised teaching schedule a negotiable item? If so, in what ways?

Will curriculum revisions place heavier demands on teachers?

How will teacher preparation and in-service programs be affected?

Will the longer year affect teacher salaries?

Can teachers accept and implement a continuous progress plan?

Will the longer year place a greater physical and mental strain on teachers?

How will teacher preparation programs and their supplementary requirements be met by area universities and colleges?

Economic Factors

Start-up Costs—those needed to initiate new programs, such as a change in materials, curriculum guides, and additional staff to get the program off the ground. Generally, these costs will be 10 percent over regular costs.

The increase of approximately 10 to 13 percent for teacher salaries.

Retirement benefits.

Cost of maintenance.

Increased transportation unless this cost is reduced.

Air conditioning as an initial cost in some climates.

The savings in classroom space. Year-round utilization of the plant reduces the needs for additional buildings that arise under the traditional plan.

Increase or reduction in textbook costs.

Increase or reduction in the number of faculty and staff.

Greater wear and tear on the faculty.

Organizational Factors

More complex scheduling patterns.

Selling the community on changing vacation patterns.

Clearly establishing the purpose of the extended year plan in the community.

Provisions by state legislation for year-round schools.

Negotiations with teacher organizations for acceptance of the change.

The question of whether the plan is to be *voluntary.*

Involvement of everyone in the planning; however, don't extend the planning period to the point of ineffectiveness.

The question of whether the need exists in the specific community for extending the school year.

If the need exists, the clear identification of that need.

Deciding whether to begin the program as an experiment in some schools, or to begin with all of the district at once.

The question of how students can transfer to other schools.

The question of the consideration of grade levels.

THE CONTINUOUS SCHOOL YEAR

There is no doubt that in the next decade many, if not a majority, of our schools will be operating within some extended-year structure. Scheduling will be considerably freer, resulting in more open school patterns. Electronic devices, such as cassettes, computer banks and retrieval systems, will all play very important and direct roles in restructuring the current school calendars.

Schools will become year-round attendance and resource centers relating closely to community, regional, and even national depots of knowledge and sociological experiences. Not only will we have an extended school year but more correctly, a *continuous school year,* an educational pattern that has been sorely needed in this country for several years.

QUESTIONS AND SUGGESTIONS FOR STUDY

1. Construct a chart providing a cost analysis comparison of the regular school year with estimated costs for each of the five types of extended-year plans discussed in this chapter. Use your school district as the source unit. Set up comparison charts for one year, two years, and five years.

2. Using various resources, list the advantages and disadvantages of the different extended-year designs as they would apply to your area.

3. Develop a rationale and public relations packet which could be used to sell a selected extended-year program to your community.

4. How might one develop a facilities analysis chart for extended-year programs?

5. Why is the extended-year calendar rapidly becoming a trend?

SELECTED REFERENCES

American Association of School Administrators. *9+ The Year-Round School.* Washington, D.C.: American Association of School Administrators, 1970.

Atlanta Public Schools. *Four-Quarter School Year.* Atlanta, Georgia: Board of Education Publication Center, 1970.

Beggs, Donald L. "The Summer Vacation—An Interruption in Learning." *Illinois Journal of Education* 60 (1969): 46-49.

Clark County School District. *The Year-Round School: A Report to the Board of School Trustees.* Las Vegas, Nevada: Clark County School District, 1968.

Ellena, William J. "Extending the School Year." *Today's Education* 58 (May 1969): 48-49.

Fitzpatrick, Dave. "Why Nova Switched to Three 70-day Trimesters." *Nation's Schools* 77 (April 1966): 4.

Friggen, Paul. "Why Not Year-Round Schools." *Reader's Digest* 74 (May 1959): 87.

Glinke, George B. *The Extended School Year: A Look at Different School Calendars.* Utica, Michigan: Utica Schools, 1970.

Hayward Unified School District. *A Feasibility Study: An Organizational and Curriculum Plan for a Four-Quarter Elementary School Year.* Hayward, California: Hayward Unified School District, 1970.

Hermasen, Kenneth L., and Gove, James R. *The Year-Round School.* Hamden, Connecticut: Linnet Books, Shoe String Press, Inc., 1971.

Ingh, Jeri. "Case for Year-Round Schools." *Reader's Digest* 89 (December 1966): 141-144.

Knezevich, Stephen J. *Administration of Public Education.* New York: Harper and Row, 1969.

Jefferson County Schools. *Signs of the Times—The Extended School Year.* Louiseville, Kentucky: Research Department of the Jefferson County Schools, 1969.

National Education Association; *The Rescheduled School Year.* Washington, D.C.: National Education Association, 1968.

Rogge, William M. *Planning a Year-Round School Operation: A Case Study of the Valley View School District 45-15 Plan.* Final Report, Project No. 0-0011, Grant No. OEG-0-70-2642 (508), Washington, D.C.: U. S. Department of Health, Education and Welfare; Office of Education, 1971.

Thomas, George Isaiah. *Extended School Year Designs.* New York: The University of the State of New York; The State Department of New York, January 1966.

University of the State of New York. *Economy and Increased Educational Opportunity through Extended School Year Programs: A Plan for a Stronger and More Economical Educational Program.* New York: New York State Education Department, 1965.

Wehmhoefer, Roy. *The Twelve-Month School Year—A Study of the Advantages and Disadvantages of the Four-Quarter System.* Chicago: Cook County Superintendent of Schools, 1968.

Whitney, H., and Piele, P. *Annotated Bibliography on Year-Round School Programs.* EDRS: ED 023199, March 1969. Microfilm.

Chapter Nine

New Horizons

The elements common to scheduling have remained constant throughout the years, but the technological processes related to them have changed noticeably during the past decade. The turning point occurred quite recently, with the impetus being a 1959 report by J. Lloyd Trump who was then Director of the Commission on the Experimental Study of the Utilization of Staff in the Secondary School. Computers had been used in schedule construction before this time, and various systems of flexible scheduling had been devised and implemented, but the concept of a *performance versus time* schedule had not been so well deployed as in Trump's experiment.

Professors Robert Oakford, Robert Bush and Dwight Allen of Stanford University were among the pioneers in using a computer to master scheduling the very complex team-teaching organizational plan—an attempt to make the school schedule as flexible as possible.

B. Frank Brown was the first to publicize the nongraded high school at Melbourne, Florida, while John Goodlad of UCLA and Robert Anderson of Harvard created a new interest in the nongraded elementary school by emphasizing a different approach from that used in the past. Other educators around the country were quick to adapt and experiment with versions of these plans as they continued the search for more effective ways to individualize learning within a mass system of education.

The 1960s may become identified as the decade of innovation and research in the schools. The growth of interest in flexible scheduling has been phenomenal, in part, because of highly efficient communications systems currently available to researchers and professional organizations.

Despite the groundswell for innovation, limited research conducted on flexible or modular scheduling has thus far produced few significant results. *Education USA,* a weekly news bulletin published by the National School Public Relations Association, summarized the conclusions drawn by 200 educators studying flexible scheduling in detail at an institute held at the University of Minnesota in 1968. A resume of this report follows:

1. There is little "solid evidence" to support it [flexible scheduling], but there is a lot of faith among its users.
2. The goal of flexible scheduling is to individualize instruction so students can learn at their own pace. A key feature is the independent or free study time for the student.
3. A major problem is motivating the students to use this "free time" wisely. Time wasters can be spotted quickly, however, and adjustments are made immediately.
4. Flexible scheduling forces teachers to change their teaching techniques and procedures. They must learn to lecture effectively, guide independent study, and remain silent in small-group discussions.
5. The teacher has a much greater role in decision-making and running the school.
6. There is no evidence to show that a student learns a subject better under flexible scheduling, but he learns more subjects and there is time for him to pursue particular interests.
7. Some feel that the value of flexible scheduling lies in its being a tool—a basis for many innovative programs.[1]

It is obvious that additional research is necessary, that the objectives of many innovative programs are difficult to assess and that the product, young men and women, is even more

---

[1]Adapted from *Education U.S.A.* (Washington, D.C.: National School Public Relations Association), April 15, 1968.

difficult to evaluate. During this decade, man has gained a greater awareness of himself than at any other time in history, and the schools have the responsibility for guiding this awareness toward the development of man as a more complete social being.

Technology has had an enormous impact upon schools in recent years. The immediate danger inherent in technology, however, is its dehumanizing effect. It is ironic that the "new" philosophy of education emphasizes learning by the individual yet assigns him a punched number on a card and proceeds to schedule his time for that day and week on a mechanized basis. It seems that the only way this student can gain attention as an individual is to mutilate his card! Schools must learn to use this new technology, but, in so doing, they must learn how to humanize the process, enabling the product of our schools to develop compassion for his fellow man. Bolding concluded his paper on technology at an area conference sponsored by the Eight State Project in this manner:

> The educational system is peculiarly specialized in the production of people, and it must never lose sight of the fact that it is producing people as ends, not as means. It is producing men, not manpower; people, not biologically generated nonlinear computers. If this principle is stamped firmly in the minds of those who guide and operate our educational system, we can afford to make a great many mistakes; we can afford to be surprised by the future; we can even afford to make some bad educational investments, because we will be protected against the ultimate mistake, which would be to make the educational system a means, not an end, serving purposes other than man himself.[2]

By 1980, a majority of our schools will be located in metropolitan areas, many of them in educational parks containing what are now termed prekindergarten grades through college or university levels. The attendance unit, regardless of the organizational pattern employed, will be designed and scheduled as a

---

[2]Kenneth Bolding, "The Economics and Financing of Technology in Education: Some Observations." In *Prospective Changes in Society by 1980* edited by Edgar L. Morphet and Charles O. Ryan (Denver, Colorado: Designing Education for the Future: An Eight State Project, 1966), p. 213.

nongraded, team-teaching, self-contained school. Special arrangements will be made to allow for independent study, to discover new information, perform certain drills, and to explore. new concepts. Consequently, the total program must be scheduled in such a way that students learn to think, to evaluate, and to utilize the increasing body of knowledge encountered in their lifetime.

One of the major challenges facing schools will be the development of a truly flexible schedule which permits time to teach, establishes a reasonable teaching load, provides a basis for using specialized skills, and allows access to unlimited resources. From the student's viewpoint, the schedule must provide a "climate for responsible individuality," the motivation to learn, and the opportunity to use acquired knowledge and skills constructively.

In such a school program, the student's schedule will vary from day to day—most of his daily schedule will be designed by the student himself. He will be permitted the freedom to select and schedule those electives he wishes to pursue on an individual basis, meeting with his teacher to establish goals and outline a work pattern and then completing the project on an independent schedule, using technological devices as learning tools, and his teachers as guides. Since student selection will also occur in elementary schools, the scheduling processes at the elementary level must be dramatically revised. Because of this "continuum" of learning, the use of technological devices will become a necessity rather than a luxury.

Perhaps the most challenging task facing the educator-technician is the humanization of the total educational process in order to effectively individualize learning within a mass system of education and to encourage man's growing awareness of himself. By accepting this challenge and experimenting with innovation, new horizons in public education will soon become a reality.

Index